THE FIRST PARTY SYSTEM:
Federalists and Republicans

PROBLEMS IN AMERICAN HISTORY

EDITOR

LOREN BARITZ

State University of New York, Albany

THE FIRST PARTY SYSTEM: Federalists and Republicans
William N. Chambers

THE LEADERSHIP OF ABRAHAM LINCOLN
Don E. Fehrenbacher

THE AMERICAN CONSTITUTION
Paul Goodman

THE AMERICAN REVOLUTION
Richard J. Hooker

THE FEDERALISTS—Creators and Critics of the Union 1780-1801
Stephen G. Kurtz

AMERICA IN THE COLD WAR
Walter LaFeber

THE ORIGINS OF THE COLD WAR, 1941-1947
Walter LaFeber

AGITATION FOR FREEDOM: The Abolitionist Movement
Donald G. Mathews

THE NATURE OF JACKSONIAN AMERICA
Douglas T. Miller

AMERICAN IMPERIALISM IN 1898
Richard H. Miller

TENSIONS IN AMERICAN PURITANISM
Richard Reinitz

THE GREAT AWAKENING
Darrett B. Rutman

WORLD WAR I AT HOME
David F. Trask

THE CRITICAL YEARS,
AMERICAN FOREIGN POLICY, 1793-1825
Patrick C. T. White

THE
FIRST PARTY SYSTEM:
Federalists and Republicans

EDITED BY

William Nisbet Chambers
Washington University

John Wiley & Sons, Inc.
New York • London • Sydney • Toronto

Library of Congress Catalogue Card Number: 70-177254

ISBN 0-471-14340-5 (cloth) ; ISBN 0-471-14341-3 (paper)

Printed in the United States of America.

10 9 8 7 6 5 4 3 2 1

SERIES PREFACE

This series is an introduction to the most important problems in the writing and study of American history. Some of these problems have been the subject of debate and argument for a long time, although others only recently have been recognized as controversial. However, in every case, the student will find a vital topic, an understanding of which will deepen his knowledge of social change in America.

The scholars who introduce and edit the books in this series are teaching historians who have written history in the same general area as their individual books. Many of them are leading scholars in their fields, and all have done important work in the collective search for better historical understanding.

Because of the talent and the specialized knowledge of the individual editors, a rigid editorial format has not been imposed on them. For example, some of the editors believe that primary source material is necessary to their subjects. Some believe that their material should be arranged to show conflicting interpretations. Others have decided to use the selected materials as evidence for their own interpretations. The individual editors have been given the freedom to handle their books in the way that their own experience and knowledge indicate is best. The overall result is a series built up from the individual decisions of working scholars in the various fields, rather than one that conforms to a uniform editorial decision.

A common goal (rather than a shared technique) is the bridge of this series. There is always the desire to bring the reader as close to these problems as possible. One result of this objective is an emphasis on the nature and consequences of problems and events, with a de-emphasis of the more purely historiographical issues. The goal is to involve the student in the reality of crisis, the inevitability of ambiguity, and the excitement of finding a way through the historical maze.

Above all, this series is designed to show students how experienced historians read and reason. Although health is not contagious, intellectual engagement may be. If we show students something significant in a phrase or a passage that they otherwise may have missed, we will have accomplished part of our objective. When students see something that passed us by, then the process will have been made whole. This active and mutual involvement of editor and reader with a significant human problem will rescue the study of history from the smell and feel of dust.

Loren Baritz

PREFACE

The rivalry of the Federalist and Republican parties in the United States produced what was probably the first modern party system in the world. This system appeared in the 1790s, reached maturity in the early 1800s, and then fell into decline. Sometime around 1817 or 1819, it was no more. Yet it created the base lines of party politics that have been elaborated in succeeding party systems down to the present day.

The term "party" is an old one. Its early meaning was simple: roughly, a political division within society, or a set of persons who contended against others on public questions. From Periclean Athens or Renaissance Florence to England in the seventeenth and eighteenth centuries, men entered into loose, opposing alignments in politics. The often violent and divisive conflict that resulted gave parties a bad name: they were an "evil," a threat to social order and to "just" government. Indeed, the shapers of the early American republic looked askance on parties accordingly. These older historic entities, however, were at most only primitive or transitional formations in comparison to the parties of 1800 or to the organized mechanisms of the nineteenth and twentieth centuries. Although functioning Whig and Tory parties did emerge in England during the reigns of William III and Queen Anne, they soon fell away; and they were limited in structure and depth of popular participation. The earliest modern political parties seem to have materialized in America at the end of the eighteenth century.

After the Constitution of 1789 established a truly national arena in the United States, political parties gradually took shape. The usually amorphous, state and local factions of earlier years gave way —at first, to national factions and then to national parties. The process was halting nationally, and was highly variable in the states. Yet about the year 1795 or 1796 the United States had arrived at a going, two-party system of continuing competition between Federalists and Republicans as settled political formations. The Federalists were in ascendance until the year 1800, when the Republicans became dominant in turn.

PREFACE

The past 10 or 15 years have brought a virtual renaissance in the study of early American parties. Most of the recent research has departed significantly from the early work of Charles A. Beard and his school of economic interpretation. It has emphasized, instead, party structure, political behavior, leadership patterns, issues of world politics, broad social or ideological conflict, and economic conflict. Yet the first scholars of the new wave tended to stress the national origins of parties. More recently, a number of striking studies of party formation in the states have appeared; and portions of these works are included here. There are three reasons for doing so, beyond a concern for historical panorama. First, American political parties have always been more or less federal in form, and any full understanding of national parties must include their local components. Second, several recent students have argued that party formation arose out of state as well as out of national issues or concerns; and these indigenous forces must be taken into account. Finally, the several state studies included here provide a basis for a comparative analysis of the conditions that promoted or retarded party development. This problem recurs throughout this book.

The rivalry of Federalists and Republicans marked only the beginnings of party life. Since the first party system collapsed, we have had a succession of party configurations. Thus the first "Experimental System" of the 1790s and early 1800s was followed by a second "Democratizing System" (1828 to 1854/1860), and so on through the "Civil War System" (1860 to 1893), the "Industrialist System" (1894 to 1932), and the fifth or "New Deal System," from 1932 to the present. There are ominous signs of the decadence or desuetude of major-party structures today, as critics find them increasingly unresponsive, ineffectual, or irrelevant. We may be on the eve of a sixth system, or of a no-system. An examination of the functions of the first party system and its successors, however, makes it difficult to envision how a viable, national, democratic policy could be maintained without parties of some sort. Total bureaucracy might provide a substitute for political management, but it would hardly serve democratic values.

PREFACE

To make the best use of this book, students should first read the introductions of Parts One to Five, as they provide a brief, continuing serial story of early party development. Thereafter, each introduction may be read again in relationship to the particular selections that it precedes. The limitations of space have made it necessary to eliminate footnotes from all selections. In preparing this book, I have been aided throughout by the informed judgment and cheerful endeavors of Helene Crowley, my research assistant; to her, I express my warmest appreciation. Final decisions were my own, of course, and the burden of any errors or solecisms falls on me.

WILLIAM NISBET CHAMBERS

CONTENTS

CONTENTS

THE FIRST PARTY SYSTEM:
Federalists and Republicans

PART ONE
Democracy, Deference, and Faction

Politics in the early American republic was an affair of factions rather than of parties. In some states, such as Virginia, patterns of factional politics inherited from colonial times persisted with little change. In others, new configurations emerged. Pennsylvania in the 1780s even generated something like a loose, state party system, although it soon broke down into a free-style, catch-as-catch-can factional game.

Nonetheless, one of the essential prerequisites for modern party politics was in the making. Suffrage, the right to vote, was already relatively open. A freehold in land was the common qualification, and in an agricultural society many, if not most, adult white males could meet the test. One of the side effects of the American Revolution, however, was a further extension of the vote, even though the result was a mixed bag. During the Revolutionary era only six of the thirteen states enlarged the suffrage in a clear-cut fashion, as Chilton Williamson points out, with Pennsylvania in the lead. Others retained their colonial requirements, in some cases well into the nineteenth century. A few even took a restrictive approach. In Massachusetts, and in New York and North Carolina in somewhat different form, new constitutions retained or revived the old, English Whig concept of a mixed or balanced government. The upper house of the legislature would represent men of property and substance, and the lower house would speak for the "democratical" orders of society.

Nonetheless, there were usually more voters in the woodpile than one might expect. Of the 16 states that participated in the partisan, national elections of 1796, only Vermont, Kentucky, and

Tennessee had established general, adult white male suffrage. Another five states, Pennsylvania, New Hampshire, Georgia, Delaware, and North Carolina, had opened the vote to adult, white male taxpayers on a broadly liberal basis, although in North Carolina this provision applied only to voting for the lower house of the legislature. In all five of these states, however, the tax requirements were small, compulsory, or often ignored in practice, so that an approximation to adult white male suffrage generally resulted. Five more states, Massachusetts, Connecticut, Rhode Island, New York, and Virginia, held to the old standard that a man must own a freehold in land or some other property. Two more states—New Jersey and South Carolina—admitted voters on the basis of rentals or a tax as well as land. Yet once again, where most men farmed or owned land, restrictions were not so severe as they might seem; and requirements were often loosely enforced.

The result was that a substantial majority of adult white males could vote, legally or practically. They did so, indeed, as citizens of a nation that was becoming a democratic republic rather than a full-scale democracy: it was some time before the idea became common that the right to vote should inhere in men as men instead of in property or taxpaying. It was, moreover, an adult white male republic—as minors, women, most Negroes, and Indians were simply not included: this was the eighteenth century, not the twentieth. If actual participation was often low even among white men, however, it was usually more the result of the lack of a sense of involvement or interest than of legal barriers.

In the several states, meanwhile, various forms of factional politics held sway. In many cases the interplay of factions were clearly functional enough to get public business done: New York under George Clinton was a prime example. To the ordinary citizen, however, the factional game was often confusing in the absence of clear-cut political formations, and often in the absence of any significant competition. Given the shifting character of the way the game was played, it is, perhaps, not surprising that many eligible voters often failed to play the game.

Two varieties of faction politics are described by Harry Marlin Tinkcom for Pennsylvania and Alfred F. Young for New York— neighboring states, but far from identical in their political styles. In Pennsylvania, the loose "Constitutionalist" and "Anti-Constitutionalist" proto-parties that had formed in the 1780s on the issue of the revision of the state constitution had fallen away. When the time came to elect a governor in 1790, politics was so loose and personal that it was, as a student of a later era in Pennsylvania put it, virtually "a game without rules." In New York, by contrast, a small group of leaders headed by the redoubtable Governor Clinton had already forged a broadly based faction that was able to dominate the state for years despite recurrent challenges.

In majestic Virginia, society and politics had taken on a distinctive cast from colonial times. Virginia was the largest of the states in population as well as area in 1790: Pennsylvania and New York were only third and fifth, while Massachusetts and North Carolina were second and fourth. Even so, society in the Old Dominion was remarkably homogeneous. It was overwhelmingly agricultural, with little diversity in economic or ethnic composition except for its underlying mass of disfranchised, black slaves. It was also marked by an established, descending scale of social gradations, from large planters and "long-tailed" families to lesser planters, freehold farmers, and "lesser man." Most freeholders could vote, and many did. Yet they also tended to look up to their social superiors for political leadership, to defer to the dominant planters or established families of their county as their "natural leaders." They usually, although not invariably, elected men of superior social standing to positions of power. In short, faction politics in Virginia was deference politics. Deferential systems in varying degrees, often based on different social foundations, also obtained from Massachusetts to Maryland or South Carolina. Yet as J. R. Pole shows, the persistence of deference politics in Virginia was remarkable.

The phenomenon of deference touches on the whole question of political party development, and Virginia is a good example. Broad formal access to voting is only the threshold of democracy, and is only one of the prerequisites for the growth of parties. If social structure and political culture are such that they discourage voting in an independent fashion, as Virginia political culture did, fewer men than would otherwise be the case are likely to make full use of the suffrage they enjoy. For decades to come, Virginia registered low levels of voting participation. In Pennsylvania and New York, by contrast, deference was all but dead in the first and was marked for decline in the other; and in both, society was moreover comparatively heterogeneous and complex. In both states also, comparatively elaborate and competitive party structures emerged rather quickly. Indeed, Federalist and Republican formations appeared in Virginia too before the 1790s were past. Yet Virginia's parties were somewhat slow in taking shape, and they remained circumscribed in organization and activity.

Deference on the one hand, and vigorous, mass political party action on the other might coexist for a time. In the long run, however, they would hardly prove to be compatible bedfellows.

WHO COULD PLAY THE
GAME?

1   FROM   *Chilton Williamson*
        American Suffrage from Property to Democracy

The exigencies of practical politics, the imminence of war, and the sanctions of revolutionary sentiments did not assure the incorporation of suffrage reform in all of the new constitutions of the Revolutionary era. Suffrage reform was advanced in a clearcut fashion in only six states: Pennsylvania, New Hampshire, Vermont, New Jersey, Georgia, and Maryland. In Massachusetts, suffrage change was in a reactionary direction; in New York and North Carolina, balanced forms of government were instituted, with different qualifications for electors of the upper and lower houses of the legislature. In these three states, a demand for

SOURCE. Selections from Chilton Williamson, *American Suffrage: From Property to Democracy, 1760-1860* (copyright c 1960 by Princeton University Press; Princeton Paperback, 1968), pp. 92-96,99,102-103,107-108,131-132, Reprinted by permission of Princeton University Press.

balance in government and a democratic electorate was successful. The remaining states either did not have to face the issue or resisted efforts to raise or lower the old colonial property tests. . .

The most striking, if not the most democratic, advance was made in Pennsylvania, where in 1776 Whigs, particularly of Philadelphia and the Scotch Irish interior, with the full support of the second Continental Congress overthrew the government of the old charter and wrote the most widely publicized, praised, and condemned of all the constitutions of the Revolution. . . .

Defenders of the old proprietary assembly failed to see the injustices in Pennsylvania which reformers decried. They declared their intention of defending all the charter rights of the colony, including the existing suffrage laws. To do otherwise "would be giving a fatal stab to our liberties. . . ." The subversive activities of the reformers demonstrated "what we are to expect should we suffer men professing such principles to get the direction of our affairs." One conservative claimed that many Military Associators who complained that they could not vote did not have a legitimate grievance on this score because many were apprentices, minors, or men only recently arrived in the province. He declared also that the people of New Jersey were considering following the example which Pennsylvania had set for many years of allowing nonfreeholders to vote. The only people, he said, who were denied the vote in Pennsylvania were the poor and necessitous, those who were easily bribed or coerced. . . .

The provincial conference met on June 18, 1776. It moved on the twentieth to permit all Military Associators who had paid a tax, or who had been assessed, to vote in the ensuing elections to create a new machinery of revolutionary government. Seeking to make political capital of this reform, the conference admonished the military men five days later to support the new state of affairs. "We need not remind you," it said, "that you are now furnished with new motives to animate and support your courage. You are not about to contend against the power of Great Britain in order to displace one set of villains, to make room for another."

The delegates wrote a constitution which showed the wide variety of influences stemming from the Anglo-Saxon cult and from indigenous institutions and traditions. It established a unicameral legislature, denied both the executive and the judiciary any genuine independent power, and, by so doing, established the supremacy of the legislature. The vote was granted to adult male freemen who were taxpayers. Elections by ballot were promised, and counties were divided into election districts ˋto encourage voting.

Pennsylvania Whigs were sincerely convinced that their constitution was a break with the immediate past and a great step forward in a democratic direction. However, it would seem that they exaggerated the difference between the new constitution and the old. For example, the increase in the size of the legal electorate was probably small, because about half of the freemen in the state were freeholders and a shift from a property to a taxpaying qualification enfranchised only the younger men. The real significance of the suffrage clauses of the new constitution lay in the theory, rather than in the result, of reform.

For many conservative Whigs, the Pennsylvania constitution was a prophet without honor at home and abroad. Benjamin Rush wrote that his friend, John Minton, had such hatred for it and concern for the evils which it would bring in its train that it brought on "political hypochondriases which put an end to his life" a year or two after the Declaration of Independence. Of all Americans, John Adams could most appreciate John Minton's attitude. In Adams' opinion, the Pennsylvania constitution set a bad example for other colonies because it exemplified his definition of tyranny, a government with all power in the people, and all that power concentrated in the legislature. Adams, more than any other member of his generation, showed a comprehensive understanding of the distinction between a separation of the power to govern and a separation of the powers of government. By the first, he meant the classical separation of monarchy, aristocracy, and democracy, or mixed or balanced government. By the second, he referred to the separation of powers between an executive, a legislature, and a judiciary. In his opinion, both were the chief bulwarks against attacks on liberty and property from whatever quarter. . . .

The constitution which finally went into effect in 1780 was not an improvement [over the first] from a democratic point of view.

Its suffrage provision, for example, established a 60-pound property qualification for all state elections. . . .

As might be expected, the suffrage provisions excited considerable comment. Attacking the constitution from the standpoint of the natural rights school, the town of Stoughton declared: "Ye right of election is not a civil; but it is a natural right, which ought to be considered as a principle cornerstone in ye foundation for ye frame of Government. . . ." Northampton agreed that property should be entitled to protection in the senate, but asserted that the lower house should represent persons, as distinct from property, and should be elected as a matter of right by all ratable male polls, twenty-one years and older; and that, furthermore, the admission to the suffrage of all men who were willing to lay down their lives for their country was a matter of simple justice. . . . What was patently undemocratic in principle, however, may not have been so in practice. A strong possibility exists that the constitution did not change a situation in which adult male taxpayers were voting in both town and colony elections with the support of opinions at large.

The New York constitution of 1777 was the result of the control of the Revolution in that state by conservative Whigs. Although there were demands in the press for more democracy in New York's institutions, including suffrage, the convention chose by and large to ignore them. Typical of convention opinion, which was decisive, was that of Robert R. Livingston, who said in 1799 that he still favored not only the bicameral principle but also a balanced form of government. He approved of this form, he said, because it recognized different orders in society "as necessary to a steady government."

New York's constitution established a dual qualification for voting, intended to assure a balanced government. The election of the senators and the governor was confined to those who owned 100-pound freeholds. The assembly was to be elected by those who owned 20-pound freeholds or were 40-shilling tenants at will or for years. The suffrage clauses cut in half the freehold qualification for the lower branch of the legislature and enfranchised tenants where, as in Westchester County, they had not hitherto been permitted to vote. Under the proddings of John Jay, the convention agreed to require the use of the secret ballot in state elections after the Revolution. . . .

In Georgia, three conventions were held in 1788 and 1789 to debate the merits of more representation for the fast-growing upcountry, unicameralism, and the voting qualification. The constitution resulting from the deliberations of 1788 required a 50-pound property qualification. This was quickly criticized on the grounds that it would discourage immigration and anger war veterans as well as "benevolent" citizens who, even if rich, had faith in the lowly and humble. An advocate of property tests pointed out that those who favored representation based upon ownership of property were scarcely in a position to critize property tests for voting, that such tests would disqualify few but would nevertheless be the means of excluding from the suffrage the dregs of Europe, a single cargo of which could swamp Georgian electors at the polls. A telling illustration of the danger in allowing foreigners to vote was drawn from Montesquieu's analysis of the connection between foreign influences and the decline of Rome. Despite so spirited a defense of property tests, the constitution of 1789 conceded the vote to all free white males who had paid a tax during the preceding year. The counter-revolution in Georgia, to the extent there was one, had collapsed.

HOW THE GAME WAS
PLAYED

2 FROM *Harry Marlin Tinkcom*
Free Style Politics in Pennsylvania

In Pennsylvania the political situation was chaotic. Indeed, the loosely formed factions that had existed in the State during the past few years had all but disappeared. So nebulous had the situation become that it is almost impossible to discover any trace of general political organization whatever.

The absence of parties in the Pennsylvania of 1790 can be attributed to another contributing circumstance. There was no well-organized group of wealthy aristocrats capable of exerting an influence so powerful as to curb opposition. The old loyalists had migrated and the Revolution had further weakened the Quaker

SOURCE. Harry Marlin Tinkcom, *The Republicans and Federalists in Pennsylvania, 1790-1801: A Study in National Stimulus and Local Response,* pp. 30-41 (Harrisburg: Pennsylvania Historical and Museum Commission, 1950).

influence. Bryan, Findley, Smilie, Franklin and other advocates of democracy had done their work well.

The amorphousness of Pennsylvania politics in 1790 was well illustrated by the gubernatorial election held in that year. The political dominance enjoyed by the conservatives on State issues since 1787 was not overwhelming; neither was their partisan majority. Those facts were emphasized by the constitutional convention, summoned at their behest, in a body of organic law which was frankly a compromise effort. The real test of their superiority would lie in their ability to install a man of their own choice in the Governor's chair. As it turned out they failed to do so, for the man eventually selected was as much of a compromise as the constitution itself. . . .

Some members of Pennsylvania's congressional delegation calmly assumed that the task of selecting a candidate would naturally fall upon them. For intimate information on the schemes and plans they concocted we are indebted to Senator [William] Maclay. Nostalgic for his beloved Susquehanna, rheumatic and often only painfully mobile, he kept his sensitive ears to the ground and his vitriolic pen handy. Suspicious and distrustful of the group he referred to as the "Philadelphia junto," in which he included [Thomas] Fitzsimons, [Robert] Morris and [George] Clymer, he busied himself in ferreting out any schemes that might be afoot. On February 4, 1790, he confessed a doubt as to whom the junto would support. But he was certain that it would select someone who would "be their tool."

As time went on, the plotting and conniving progressed. On February 8, 1790, Morris presented a memorial to the Senate requesting the appointment of commissioners "to inquire into his conduct while financier [of the Revolution], and mentioning his unsettled accounts as a partner of Willing and Morris, which were in train of settlement." Frederick Muhlenberg told Maclay the Philadelphians had agreed that Morris' memorial should be presented as the first step in clearing the way for his candidacy. Fitzsimons, who had informed Muhlenberg of the plan to boost Morris, was strongly opposed to Thomas Mifflin. As President of the Executive Council and a popular figure throughout the State, Mifflin would be a difficult man to defeat. But if he were elected,

Fitzsimons declared, "they would be worse off than if no new constitution had been made."

Morris disapproved of Bingham as well as of Colonel Samuel Miles, a former Censor and Revolutionary patriot whose candidacy Maclay had heard advocated. But he was especially opposed to Mifflin. While discussing the latter with Maclay in the Senate, Morris deprecated Mifflin's appointments as President of the Executive Council. Then, with an oblique reference to Maclay's interest in public lands, he mentioned the Surveyor Generalship. "You should have had that office," he said.

At the same time Morris spoke in favor of Arthur St. Clair as Governor. The latter had reason to be grateful not only for Morris' support, later openly given, but for a past favor. While serving as Superintendent of Finance during the Revolution, Morris had advanced sums of money from his own resources to certain needy army officers. St. Clair had been one of them.

Frederick A. Muhlenberg, Speaker of the House, also with an eye on the Governor's chair, was much troubled by some news sent to him in April, 1790, by political friends. It seemed that the "aristocrats in Philadelphia would support Mifflin instead of him. To Maclay he mournfully reflected on the inadequate return those "aristocrats had always made to him for his engaging the Germans to support their measure.". . .

The Pennsylvania delegation to Congress had been in the habit of holding dinner meetings at Simon's tavern in New York [briefly the national capital] to discuss current affairs. At one held early in May, 1790, Fitzsimons declared that it was expected that they should nominate a candidate for Governor. Maclay quickly interposed some remarks on the weather and succeeded in postponing a discussion. But after Scott, Hiester and Peter Muhlenberg left, Fitzsimons returned to his subject. Morris then made his wishes known by stating that although he was not unaware of the honor of his senatorial office he would, if elected Governor, discharge his duties impartially. Since Mifflin was a "very improper man," he hoped that "they would create opposition to him." After Muhlenberg declared himself in agreement with Morris, the group decided to unite in an effort to defeat Mifflin. "Mr. Morris, by way of finishing the business, addressed himself to the Speaker. 'May you or I be Governor.'"

Judging from the repeated mention of Mifflin's name and the concerted effort made to defeat him, it is evident that the inner congressional circle of Pennsylvania regarded his candidacy as a serious challenge. As a matter of fact, his supporters had not been idle. In June, 1790, James Hutchinson, a Philadelphia doctor who was later to take a leading part in the election of 1792, was quite confident of Mifflin's success. In a letter to Albert Gallatin he expressed great satisfaction at hearing that Washington and Fayette counties were so favorable to Mifflin. He made certain that the "aristocrats of this city" (Philadelphia) would oppose him. He had not yet learned who would be placed in opposition. But he did mention the possible candidacies of Frederick Muhlenberg and Morris, with the belief that Morris would be chosen. It is to be noted that Muhlenberg's correspondents and Hutchinson conflicted in their opinions as to whom the "aristocrats" really favored.

Not all the self-appointed governor-makers were Congressmen. Samuel Bryan, office seeker, also decided to try his hand at the interesting game by advocating the candidacy of his father George, ardent defender of the Constitution of 1776, and a Judge of the State Supreme Court. In May, 1790, he informed Albert Gallatin that although the "whigs" in eastern Pennsylvania had decided to support Mifflin because he was the best man they "could carry," they had but recently discovered that the "dormant spirit of the old whigs" was reviving so vigorously that there was a very good likelihood of electing a more acceptable man. To sponsor Mifflin was "weakness itself," for there was "not a half-penny difference between Morris, Mifflin or Muhlenberg." His candidacy had inspired indifference and listlessness. Therefore they had decided to boost his father George, a proposal that was meeting with a fine response in Bucks, Montgomery, Chester and Northampton counties. An energetic campaign was being conducted in those counties with every promise of success.

The name of the junto candidate was not publicly announced until September, 1790. Before the Constitutional Convention finally adjourned on the second of that month several of its members combined with a few assemblymen to select a candidate. The results of this caucus were declared in an electioneering broadside a few days later. Over the signatures of Thomas

Fitzsimons, George Clymer, Benjamin Rush, William Lewis, Robert Morris, James Wilson and Frederick A. Muhlenberg, the document warmly advocated the election of General Arthur St. Clair. After congratulating the citizens of Pennsylvania on its new constitution, the signers insisted that its promises could be made "real" if St. Clair were elected Governor. Mentioning no party names and unconcerned about specific issues, the broadside stressed the personal qualifications of St. Clair. He was patriotic, well-mannered, honest, informed and possessed of considerable military talent. After listing the candidate's estimable qualities, the signers struck a significant note when they pointed out that "he possesses the confidence of the President of the United States, and of course will not fail to use it for the important purpose of maintaining a constant harmony between the State of Pennsylvania and the Executive power of the National Government."

Thomas Mifflin was born of Quaker parentage in Philadelphia in 1744. After graduating at the age of sixteen from the College of Philadelphia, he entered a business partnership with his brother George. As an ardent defender of colonial rights he opposed the Stamp Act, and subsequently took part in the First Continental Congress. Although he preferred active battle participation, in which he later displayed unusual personal bravery, he was appointed quartermaster general in 1775, a rank he held, with one brief interlude, until 1778. When his administration of the quartermaster's department was censured as being inefficient, he resigned from the army. He then served in the Continental Congress from 1782 to 1784. He was elected president of that body in 1783.

For a connection between Mifflin's war record and his candidacy for the governorship reference should be made to the following. It will be recalled that the circular issued by the junto claimed that their candidate St. Clair possessed "the confidence of the President of the United States." Since St. Clair's sponsors had long recognized Mifflin as a formidable opponent, this phrase may have been a veiled allusion to the latter's supposed dislike of Washington. But any deeper interpretation of the phrase can rest only on the assumption that his comtemporaries were aware of the historically alleged jealousy that he felt for the commander-in-chief. It has been said that as quartermaster general he aided

General Horatio Gates in his plots. According to Bernhard Knollenberg there were contemporary rumors to the effect that Mifflin was hostile to Washington, but Mifflin "denied such hostility. . .and there is no substantial evidence in support of the charge." William Rawle, the elder, a contemporary, was sure that Mifflin was completely innocent of any plot to remove Washington from command.

Mifflin had the natural politician's ability to get along with a great variety of personalities and temperaments. Adept at social amenities and of an amiable disposition, he won friends easily. "In person," said William Rawle, "he was remarkably handsome, though his stature did not exceed five feet eight inches. His frame was athletic, and seemed capable of bearing much fatigue. His manners were cheerful and affable. His elocution open, fluent, and distinct."

His name was placed before the electorate by a number of nominating meetings held in September and October. The *Pennsylvania Packet,* a Philadelphia newspaper, published the results of meetings held in the city and in Chester and Montgomery counties. The identity of these nominating groups from the standpoint of party affiliation past or future cannot be determined by their use of party labels, for none was announced. No mention was made of the old Constitutionalist or Anti-Constitutionalist groups or of the Federalists or Anti-Federalists. With what seemed to be a studied vagueness, the participants in those gatherings referred to them as meetings of "numerous" and "respectable" citizens or as "freeholders" and "electors." At a Philadelphia meeting on October 9, 1790, presided over by Charles Biddle, Mifflin was nominated along with several candidates for the Assembly. The men selected were Jacob Hiltzheimer, Lawrence Seckle, Francis Gurney, Richard Wells and William Bingham. All had been prominently identified with the Anti-Constitutionalist group, and a few were later to play conspicuous roles as Federalists. This was also true of the principals behind St. Clair's candidacy in Philadelphia.

When the junto came into the open with its candidate, the public response was not very satisfactory. Indeed, the electorate was so apathetic to St. Clair that in less than a week after the letter advocating his election appeared in the *Packet* on September

18, 1790, at least one of his supporters began to despair of success. This was no less a figure than Thomas Fitzsimons, an important leader in the campaign. On September 24 he mournfully observed that opposition to Mifflin was extremely feeble, and what little there was only served to make him stronger. He supposed therefore that "we must submit to the consequences." Mifflin had associated himself "with the Constitutionalists" and Fitzsimons thought it likely that most of the State would fall into his hands. Such an outcome would be "vexatious" but not "as prejudicial" now as formerly. He was convinced that a Mifflin victory would produce another combination.

The junto candidate was reluctant to run for the governorship, but he did so out of gratitude to his Philadelphia friends. He was happy, he told Fitzsimons, to have the approbation of "men who stand foremost in the community for wisdom probity and patriotism." Admitting that Mifflin had made a large number of friends, St. Clair, nevertheless, discovered that his own candidacy was "relished in every part of the country I passed thro." He had learned from a political informant that William Findley was busily engaged in gathering votes for Mifflin in Westmoreland County. "They" planned to alter Findley's behavior though, by hinting that "they" had another person in mind for the next congress. As to the success of their maneuver, St. Clair guessed that if Findley felt himself in danger he would "come round, if not—it will only make him more assiduous—I have however very little doubt that the counties on his side of the mountain will be divided in spite of the exertione he can make."

But Findley, the shrewd prognosticator, had already made up his mind. He thought Mifflin would be the successful candidate. He was right, but the extent of Mifflin's victory must have surprised the westerner, for he thought the contest would be close.

Far from being close, the election was a great triumph for Mifflin. In fact, his margin of victory was so overwhelming that it was virtually no contest.

When all the results were in it was found that he had won by a vote of 27,725 to a mere 2,802 for his opponent. A third candidate, Charles Thomson, received two votes. Not one county gave a majority to St. Clair.

In evaluating the election results, it would seem that the issue

was determined not by party organization or alignments but by
personalities. Mifflin, widely known and popular throughout the
State, was more than a match for an opponent who was less
familiar to the electorate. As a westerner, however, despite his
backing by the "Morris" or junto clique, St. Clair made a
relatively better showing in his section than in any other part of
the State or in the State generally. It is certainly true that Mifflin
must have received many votes from the old Constitutionalist
party, but in view of his overwhelming majority the same would
hold true for the former Anti-Constitutionalists. As a popular
figure then, he transcended old party alignments and further
blurred the already confused political picture. That he had the
support of many of the old Constitutionalist leaders is undoubted.
Findley, Gallatin, James Hutchinson and Samuel Bryan all
favored him. Findley certainly enjoyed Mifflin's closest confidence,
and he was to continue to do so for many years. Samuel Bryan was
of the opinion that Mifflin had emancipated "himself from the
servile thraldom of a junto" that would permit no "deviation from
their monopolising dictates. . . ." He referred of course to the
Morris-Fitzsimons group. Mifflin had been elected, Bryan declared, through "the patronage and zealous support of the independent part of the Community, aided by a concurrence of highly
favorable incidents."

3 FROM   *Alfred F. Young*
           The Clintonians in New York

On June 10, 1789, George Clinton walked from the governor's
mansion in New York City to the home of Rufus King, recently
settled in the city from his native Massachusetts and even more
recently elected a member of the New York Assembly. King was
not at home. The governor left his card and returned the next day
but King was out again. On June 12 King returned the visit, and
Clinton moved quickly to his purpose: sounding out the well-
known Federalist on accepting anti-Federalist support for a seat in
the United States Senate.

Clinton's puzzling offer is explicable only in the context of New
York's tangled political history. After dominating New York
politics as governor since 1777, George Clinton had suffered a
series of setbacks that left him with his back to the wall: the
unanticipated Federalist victory at Poughkeepsie the previous
summer which had secured the state's ratification of the federal
Constitution; the subsequent stalemate in the state legislature over
the choice of federal senators as a result of a split between the
"adopting" and "nonadopting" anti-Federalists; and Clinton's
near-defeat in the recent gubernatorial campaign after going all
but unchallenged in the three elections since 1777.

In his extraordinary interview with King, Clinton began by
explaining the controversy in the legislature over the selection of
senators, pointing out why Melancton Smith and John Lansing
would not or could not be the anti-Federalist choice. When
Clinton asked King whom he had heard spoken of as candidates,
King named besides Lansing, Robert Yates, another anti-Federalist, and Philip Schuyler, Robert R. Livingston, James Duane, and

SOURCE. Alfred F. Young. *—The —Democratic —Republicans —of —New —York: —the
—Origins —1763-—1797,* pp. 3-6, 8-9, 34-41, 54-56 (Chapel Hill: University of North
Carolina Press, 1967). Reprinted by permission of the University of North Carolina
Press, the author, and the Institute of Early American History and Culture.

Richard Morris, leaders of the conservative Whig nationalists during the Revolution and now leaders of the state's Federalists. Each of the Federalists was a member of New York's unique landed aristocracy, the estate holders of the Hudson Valley: Schuyler was the most powerful figure of the Albany area; Duane was son-in-law of the upper manor Livingstons, owner of Duanesburgh in his own right, and the mayor of New York; Livingston was chancellor and the head of the Clermont or lower manor branch of his family; Richard Morris, associate justice of the supreme court, was son of the late Lewis Morris, lord of the manor of Morrisania of Westchester.

Deftly, Clinton explained his objection to each of the men mentioned by King. He "questioned whether any gentlemen in the state judiciary ought to take a share in the national Legislature, that this might be confounding the judiciary and Legislative Department," a comment that clearly eliminated Judges Morris, Livingston, and Yates. Lansing could not serve for personal reasons. Then, with a mounting impatience, Clinton warmed to a history lesson for the newcomer to New York politics:

". . .besides that it had uniformly been his opinion that the Offices of Great Power should not all be concentrated in a certain party, or family association--that their abilities and wealth already gave them great influence, and that the addition of great Offices to the entire exclusion of other characters might endanger the public liberty--That he was desirous that they should be allowed their reasonable share according to their abilities, and that he would pay a proper consideration to their property, but that such allowance should be a distinct thing from a monopoly of the public office."

This took care of Schuyler, Livingston, and Duane. Duane, Clinton knew, considered it his right to be chosen senator, but no man had such a right. Who then should be senator? "Some Persons," Clinton said, "had thought that there should be a mercantile character" in the Senate but "it was a little difficult to find one in all points suitable."

Clinton was ready to be direct: what about King? His visitor was properly coy; he was "but lately an inhabitant of the state"; many of "the old and very reputable citizens would claim it as their right"; he had no desire to stir up controversy. Clinton dismissed King's objections one by one. When King brought up Duane's name again, Clinton replied heatedly, revealing his conception of his own role in New York politics. Before the Revolution, he said, "there were two great families or parties named Delancey and Livingston" in the state; "now the case was different," for "all the great opulent families were united in one confederacy." His "politicks" were "to keep a constant eye to the measures of this combination."

As if to clinch his argument, Clinton ended by pointing out who had put forward King's name: "some gentlemen from the country" in the legislature, the men he might have added who for more than a decade had been the backbone of Clinton's support in his battles with "the great opulent families." They were "men of sound judgement," the Governor explained, defensively, "but not used to public speaking," and they resented the ridicule heaped upon them by polished orators. They would be gratified, the Governor suggested to the new assemblyman, by having the legislature meet occasionally, not in New York—the sophisticated metropolis, the center of Federalism—but at Poughkeepsie, or the even more bucolic hamlet of Esopus, near Kingston. The Governor perhaps was drifting. King, sensing that Clinton had exhausted his purpose, excused himself. The interview was over.

Clinton's history lesson had laid bare the antagonisms of a quarter-century of New York politics: the domination of colonial political life by "the great opulent families"; the rivalry between the two greatest, the Delanceys and the Livingstons, which dominated colonial politics from the 1750's until the strife of the era of Revolution ushered in new political movements; the conflict during the Revolution between the "popular" and conservative wings of the Whig party; Clinton;s unexpected elevation to the governorship and his forging of the instruments of power. What Clinton had not discussed with King was implicit in his story: the harsh conflict between tenant and landlord which thrust across the better-known political struggles; the elimination in the wake of the Revolution of not only the Delanceys but also a wing of the landed and mercantile aristocracy which made it possible for "new men" to gain political and economic power; and finally, the quest of a frustrated aristocracy to regain as nationalists and Federalists the prize that had eluded them as conservative Whigs. All this, and more, was in the marrow of the men who were making New York politics as Clinton's interview with King signaled the end of an era.

* * *

What George Clinton and his contemporaries took for granted about the politics of colonial New York was made a commonplace among historians by Carl Becker in his classic monograph in 1909. "A small coterie of closely related families," wrote Becker, "was able in large measure to control provincial politics."

Landlord dominance of their own bailiwicks was a fact of life [before the Revolution], not immutable, but sufficient to discourage most men from challenging it. The proprietors of the three tracts entitled to send representatives to the assembly, Colden explained, "are become Hereditary Members." "The owners of the other great Pattents being Men of the greatest Opulence in the several Countys where the Tracts are, have sufficient influence to be perpetually Elected for these Countys." The lord of Livingston Manor claimed that normally he could "carry" four hundred or so tenant voters. Between the Livingstons and Van Rensselaers, it was said that "it is in their power to determine every election in the county of Albany." In every county south of Albany along the east bank of the Hudson there were other large estate holders to be reckoned with: in Dutchess, the lower manor Livingstons, allied with the Beekmans, and the owners of the Beverly Robinson and Philipse estates; in Westchester, the Philipses and Van Cortlandts, who together with the "manors" of Fordham, Pelham, Morrisania, and Scarsdale occupied two thirds of the county; in Manhattan, the Delanceys. To the west along the Mohawk was the powerful Sir William Johnson family; to the northeast several lesser estate holders. Only in Orange and Ulster counties on the west bank of the Hudson and Suffolk on eastern Long Island were yeomen farmers numerous enough to set the tone for their counties. It was these counties and sometimes Dutchess and Tryon which sent Colden's "common farmers" to the assembly.

The landed gentry could not expect to have their candidates automatically elected; they often had to court and treat the voters, just as did their better-known Virginia brethren. Bribery was common, and even so, more than a few elections went awry. But to Abraham Yates, stormy petrel of Albany County politics, New

York's assembly districts resembled England's rotten boroughs: "for what material difference is there," he asked, "whether one elector by his own voice sends a member to Parliament or a manor settled with a hundred or a thousand tenants, under the influence of one person," sends a member to the assembly. Men like ·Yates, one-time sheriff and later a bitter enemy of "the manor lords," were advocates of electoral reforms, especially of a written ballot, by means of which Yates said, quoting Harrington, "no man in this way need fear the disobliging of his landlord, customer or benefactor."

* * *

George Clinton, the dominant figure in New York politics of the 1780's, like democratic leaders of other times and places, epitomized in many ways the background and aspirations of his followers; in him their characteristics were writ large. Clinton had a better start in life than most of those in his party. He "had noble blood in his veins," his biographer asserts, as a "direct descendant of Henry, the second Earl of Lincoln." "He was also a distant cousin of that other George Clinton, the son of the Sixth Earl of Lincoln who was the governor of the province of New York from 1743 to 1753." His father acquired land, became a surveyor and a farmer, and through his connections with the royal governor, first judge of Ulster County.

As the crisis with Britain deepened, Clinton earned the reputation of a staunch Whig in the Livingston party. Elected a delegate to the Continental Congress in 1775, he was "silent in general and wants (when he does speak) the influence to which he is entitled." At the outbreak of hostilities he chose to fight rather than make laws. Appointed a brigadier general in the militia, he contributed more in the opening months "to the waging of the war than any other general officer from New York with the exception of Schuyler."

He had many of the attributes of a democratic politician, not least of which was his ability to wield patronage. George Clinton did not initiate the "spoils system" in New York but he did not need either his nephew, DeWitt Clinton, or Thurlow Weed to teach him the uses of appointments, land grants, and political favors to further his "interest." Anyone familiar with the techniques of the royal governors knew that, and the constitution by making the governor the head of a Council of Appointment and vesting in it the royal governor's power to select judges to the supreme court, the mayors of New York and Albany, county sheriffs, clerks, judges, and other minor officials made the governor the inevitable cynosure of pressure for the "loaves and fishes."

Clinton's popular reputation always rested fundamentally on his role in the Revolution. The judgement [Alexander] Hamilton made in 1777—that "General Clinton is an excellent officer, the people have Confidence in him, will once act with zeal and Serve with Spirit and perserverence under him"—was never erased by all of Hamilton's later propaganda. As one soldier, an active Republican at Plattsburgh, later recalled, "he led me into military rank when I was but a boy—I have shared the perils of the field by his side . . . I have admired him for his simplicity of manners, ease of access, decision and firmness." Thousands of others in New York had the same emotional experience. In the opinion of the historian who has studied the governors throughout the colonies his administration as wartime governor was one of the best. All of this added up to the record that his followers would emblazon on his banners in many campaigns: George Clinton, the "tried and tested Whig," "old seventy-six," George Clinton, "the publican general."

* * *

Conservatives were obsessed not so much with George Clinton as with the "new men" he helped raise to power. In the spring of 1782, as Alexander Hamilton surveyed the New York political scene in a report to his new chieftain and mentor, Robert Morris, he clearly recognized two sides to George Clinton. He had, on the one hand, wrote Hamilton, "declined in popularity, partly from a defect of qualifications for his station and partly from causes that do him honor—the vigorous execution of some necessary laws that bore hard upon the people, and severity of discipline among the militia." On the other hand, said Hamilton, "the preservation of his place is an object to his private fortune as well as to his ambition; and we are not to be surprised, if instead of taking a lead in measures that contradict a prevailing prejudice, however he may be convinced of their utility, he either flatters it or temporizes; especially when a new election approaches."

By contrast, to paint the portraits of the leading politicians in the legislature, Hamilton dipped his pen in acid.

Hamilton was lamenting what was in effect a shift in the political center of gravity in New York from one class to another. That such a shift did indeed take place has recently been verified by Jackson T. Main's careful comparison of the postwar assembly and senate with the prewar assembly and council as to occupations, wealth, and social origins. The assembly, Main concludes:

". . .differed from the old in many respects. The voters selected fewer townspeople. In the 1769 Assembly some 57 per cent of the members had been engaged primarily in a nonagricultural occupation; by 1785 the proportion had been halved. Farmers, exclusive of large landowners, had made up 25 per cent of the total in 1769; now they furnished about 42 per cent. In contrast, one half of the 1769 legislators had been merchants and lawyers, but now such men held less than one third of the seats. Similarly the proportion of wealthy members dropped from 43 per cent to 15 per cent, whereas the ratio of men of moderate means increased from probably one seventh to nearly one half. New York's elite families, which had contributed ten out of twenty-eight Assemblymen in 1769, contributed the same number in 1785, but in a House twice as large. Meanwhile the number of men who had started without any local family background, newcomers to New York, increased from two to twenty-three. In general, the yeoman-artisan "middle class" which in colonial days had furnished a half-dozen members, now actually had a majority of the legislature."

The senate had also changed drastically. Among the senators who served from 1777 to 1787, descendants of prominent old families held from one-fourth to one-third of the seats compared to three-fourths of the provincial council. The number of men newly risen was about the same, but the greatest change was in the appearance of a large bloc of men comprising about 40 per cent of the total from old respectable families but not of the elite. Wealth was still noticeable, but where the old council was composed almost completely of wealthy men, in the new senate about 40 per cent were wealthy, about 36 per cent were well-to-do, and 25 per cent were of moderate property. An occupational shift also took place. The council was dominated by merchants, large landholders, and lawyers; about a third of the postwar senate was made of large landholders and a third of farmers.

* * *

The politics of the Clintonians—the means by which the Governor and his circle consolidated an "interest"—are best summed up by an apt phrase of George Dangerfield: they represented "the politics of opportunity" as opposed to the "politics of privilege." Clinton stood for what another analyst of his philosophy has called "the middle class democracy of New York State." He was neither a "radical," nor a "pure agrarian," nor a "reformer," although historians have pinned all these labels on him.

CLINTON: PRE-
SERVATION OF
PROPERTY RTS.

Clearly Clinton never stood for "levelling principles." The aim of government, he told the legislature, was to preserve "lives, liberties and estates." "The security of property," he said, "forms one of the strongest bonds of society; too much care cannot be taken to preserve and strengthen it." The virtues he prized were those of the northern states, "where freedom, independence, equality and frugality are natural to the climate and soil." Southern slaveholders, and by implication Hudson Valley estate holders, were men with "a passion for aristocratic distinction" who "know not what it is to acquire property by their own toil, nor to economize with the savings of industry."

There had to be opportunity, according to Clinton, for men whose "manners and fortunes bear a more equal resemblance" to those of the citizenry at large to hold office. Encouraging education therefore was "the peculiar duty of the government of a free state where the highest employments are open to citizens of every rank." For the same reason there also had to be adequate compensation for public officials, "now that a field is open for the display of talents and industry"—the twist in the phrase, avoiding Jefferson's "talents and virtue," was characteristically middle class. Only then would those who "have a prospect of advancing themselves and their families in private life" be able to hold office.

There also had to be opportunity to acquire land, although it must be said that Clintonian policies favored the speculator rather than the settler. Clinton looked forward, he told the legislature, to "a speedy settlement" of the vast interior by pioneers and endorsed the idea of a tax on "large tracts of uncultivated lands" in the hands of "absentees and aliens," which, had it passed the legislature, would have forced one body of land engrossers to disgorge, but he also looked upon the public land as a source of revenue and drew a distinction between the promoter who presumably would sell land quickly and the unproductive land speculator. This approach led him to distribute confiscated Tory land to speculators as well as farmers, to open the state land to speculators in the late 1780's and to distribute in 1791 some 5,000,000 acres on a scale more lavish than that of any royal governor.

Clinton is not understood as a "radical," even if that term is modified to be "no violent radical." His postwar record on the tenant question continued that of the war years. He showed his colors in the acid test of the 1780's, Shay's Rebellion. The uprising in Massachusetts in 1786 immediately across the border from Albany County frightened landlords, expecially after fugitives escaped into eastern New York. Clinton excoriated the "horrid and unnatural rebellion," offered a reward for the capture of the leaders, enjoined New Yorkers from aiding them, and ordered three regiments of Dutchess and Columbia militia to eastern New York. He personally made his way up from New York City at three in the morning on a wintry February night to direct the operations that dispersed the refugee rebels and impressed the local tenants with the might of the state. Clinton's followers were at pains to point out they were not "Shaysites."

As he was not a "radical" neither did he typify "the pure agrarian" in economics. Characteristically in a formal message to the legislature he took note of the fact that "the toils of the Husbandman have been amply awarded by a fruitful season and a plentiful harvest." But it was not merely a political gesture when he added that "while we are pursuing agriculture as our first object, commerce and manufactures also deserve our attention." Bitter because American trade was being thrown "into the hands of persons styling themselves or acting among us on the disguise of British subjects," he advocated tonnage discrimination by the state against British ships, tariff protection against British imports, and "particular encouragement" for New Yorkers' budding trade with India. To encourage native manufactures, he favored state bounties and, later, loans. He was not opposed on principle to the state's chartering banks-it depended on who was asking for the charter. And he never encouraged an inflationary currency. Clintonians were responsible in 1786 for issuing   200,000 in currency backed by land, which was as stable as the colonial

"Land Bank" on whose precedent it was based.

Clinton, furthermore, was only a mild reformer. He advocated public support for education, yet in the 1780's was satisfied with the legislature's formal and parsimonious response to his appeal. Personally, he was anti-slavery; he even served a one-year term as vice-president of the Manumission Society in New York City. Officially, he avoided the issue which would have alienated the small slaveholders of the Hudson Valley who voted for him.

Hamilton's electioneering gibe in 1789—"I do not recollect a single measure of public utility since the peace, for which the state is indebted to its chief magistrate"—was not as damning as he thought. Clinton's program, by design, was essentially negative. The lodestar of his policy was to avoid any measure which might burden his agrarian constituents with taxes; hence Clintonians were indifferent to any program entailing large-scale expenditures, and weighed any new measure by the standard of how much revenue it might bring into state coffers.

4   FROM   *J. R. Pole*

Deference Politics in Virginia

Thomas Jefferson, when compiling his *Notes on Virginia*, looked into the suffrage question and came to the gloomy conclusion that the majority of men in the state who paid taxes and fought did not possess the right to vote. Estimates—not of voters, but of tithables and of freeholders paying quitrents—had been drawn up and transmitted at earlier dates by Governor Dinwiddie (1756) and Auditor-General John Blair (1773) as information for the Board of Trade. To these surveys must now be added the much more

SOURCE. J. R. Pole, *Political Representation in England and the Origins of the American Republic,;* pp. 146-51, 153-5, 161-3 (London: The Macmillan Company, 1966). Reprinted by permission of St. Martin's Press, Inc., The Macmillan Co. of Canada Ltd., and the author.

detailed evidence of the distribution of property and of the actual exercise of the suffrage disclosed by the assiduous researches of Professor and Mrs. [Robert E.] Brown. The effect is certainly to make Jefferson's findings appear excessively gloomy.

The character of a suffrage franchise based on property will obviously be affected by economic opportunity. The prevailing factors of cheap land, a propulation that grew without growing faster than the resources of the economy, and the all-important basis of a labour force of slavery and indentured servitude, combined to liberate a high proportion of the white population to the extent of becoming owners of freehold or leasehold property in land. The effect, taken together with the laxity and uncertainty in the enforcement of the election laws from place to place, was to yield an effective voting force which could rise to over sixty per cent of the white male population of adults and which under pressure could be pushed considerably higher. When elections were closely contested the candidates, who themselves were always members of the gentry, showed a keener interest in swelling their support by agreeing to a liberal interpretation of the franchise than in a strict insistence on the letter of the law: at least until the election was lost. The bitterness of defeat often led disappointed candidates to challenge the return and dispute the election before the House of Burgesses

The evidence of suffrage practices in different counties under varying local interpretations of the law is bound to be inconclusive. Men who acquired enough property to enable them to vote many often have spent a fair portion of their lives getting it. Given the basic condition that the economy was built on the backs of a vast, unenfranchised labour force, the most important thing to grasp is the trend rather than specific local conditions. "By common consent and contrary to law," concludes the most distinguished historian of the subject [Charles S. Sydnor], "a local movement toward universal manhood suffrage was on foot. It was a period of ambitious activity, involving men of all ranks in prospects of enrichment in the west. The gentry of Virginia, who were not a European aristocracy, strove with some success to emulate the character of an eighteenth-century oligarchy: but it was not one of ancient and effete families clinging to power against the tide—on the contrary, it was vigorous, furiously ambitious, and tolerably open to recruitment. The "open" side of this society did not long survive the American Revolution; and without the Revolution it is at least possible that its mood might have been reversed even sooner. The facts that property was widespread and relatively easy to acquire did nothing to liberalise the legislators towards those who fell outside the circle of property owners, or who might do so at some future period. The law based on property could be and often was permissively administered. But a marked and effective restriction could be brought about by a mere change in the mood of the administration, without any change in the principle of the law. In fact, no new restrictions had been enacted in Virginia when, even before Jefferson's Republican Party had won a national election, bitter complaints against suffrage restriction began to reach the House. Universal suffrage was assuredly not the basis of Virginian political society when Jefferson led his party to victory in the Federal government in 1800; and that party did nothing to make the suffrage more liberal in his own state.

The jocular familiarity of elections in Virginia both before and after the Revolution, the occasionally large turnout of voters and the keen competition between candidates give its politics an attractive air of republican vitality. In fact, however, this appearance can be deeply deceptive. The role of the electorate was extremely circumscribed. The voters were called into action to elect a new House of Burgesses in the colonial period about once every three years; they knew little of issues, had practically no opportunity to read political debates, and were very rarely called on to make decisions that would determine between alternative policies. They formed an essentially deferential electorate who willingly acknowledged the leadership and authority of the gentry. Membership of the gentry was a condition which conferred the right to participate in politics; an attempt to participate might be an ambitious man's test of whether his social standing was recognised by his county neighbours. In face of keen competition, the laws and conventions which precluded active advocacy of one's own cause began to break down; the disgraceful practice of 'electioneering' gradually became a painful necessity—and never ceased, for its beneficiaries, to be a feast of entertainment. If the suffrage was fairly wide shortly before the Revolution, it was a suffrage that did not threaten the existing social leadership; and long afterwards, in the era of the Republican Party, the politics of Virginia continued in large measure to be dominated by a recognised upper class; the Republican Party of Virginia represented the mobilisation of that leadership in the interest of capturing the Federal government.

The key to this Republican leadership after the emergence of the national issues on which political parties were built up, was the continued claim of the Republican gentry to the loyalty and support of the freeholders. When personal competition, which had begun to open the system, gave place to competition on divisive issues such as Jay's Treaty of 1794, it became all the more important for Republican leaders to stand together, and to maintain the unity of that social fabric of which they had always stood as the recognised 'heads. Their success in this enterprise enabled them to withstand the pressure for a more democratic suffrage and for a reapportionment of seats in the Assembly for another generation. For heirs and bearers of the amateur tradition, it was no mean political achievement.

The crucial event in any system of representation is the election itself. The procedure changed very little in Virginia throughout the eighteenth century and its main features could still be recognised in the days of Jackson. For all concerned an election was an important and exciting event. The poll was not movable, and voters had to come up for the day, often passing a night on the journey accommodated by one of the candidates or his supporters. To open the proceedings in the court house the sheriff, after reading aloud the writ, took his place behind the long table, at each end of which sat the candidates. If, as usually happened, a poll was required because the result could not be decided by shout, the electors filed up, one by one, announced their votes and were then, as a rule, entitled to be thanked by the gentleman of their choice. "Sir, I shall treasure that vote as long as I live"; "Sir, may you live a thousand years," were acceptable epithets from a grateful recipient. The elections often lasted all day, and might go on for two or three, but when the sheriff was satisfied that all the votes had been taken he might close the poll at his own discretion. Before doing so he was expected to give public warning lest any intending voters remained outside. The sheriff's return was transmitted to the House of Burgesses and would serve to certify the claim of the elected candidates to their seats. Before this, however, the effects of the rum, of which prodigious quantities were available in the taverns and the houses of the candidates' supporters, had usually begun to make themselves known. An election without a fight would have been almost as rare as a western movie without a shooting bout.

The records of voting in the colonial period do not yield any continuous series by which to establish the proportion of participants. But groups of returns from several counties, in 1755 and in 1771, together with a number of other more isolated cases, show that between 30 and 40 per cent of the adult white males frequently made their way to the polls, the proportion sometimes reaching up to 60 percent. These are high figures. Track roads, fords, and freshets often made the going difficult; and the casting of a vote for one gentleman or the other could hardly seem much inducement to such exertions. But elections were social events. The rivalry between backers of different candidates was often of the sporting kind, like that of football teams, excited but inconsequential. Meanwhile the election was a hilarious county reunion, and best of all it was a time when the mighty were forced to show fellowship with the common freeholders amid much back-slapping, rum tippling, and protestation of political reticence.

Representation in Virginia was not based on the assumption that conflicting interests called for conflicting spokesmen. Each county was supposed to have its own homogeneity of character, deriving no doubt from the earliest settlements, and the county would naturally want to be represented by its most distinguished citizen. It was no small part of communal pride. That was the nature of his distinction. In the Assembly he would be expected to confront, on equal terms, the weightiest men of other communities. Such gentlemen were not expected to vulgarise themselves by making crude promises of material betterment. Only men striving for advancement adopted such ungentlemanly methods.

Virginia counties, especially those in the Tidewater and Piedmont, were politically dominated by their magnates. Issues seldom entered elections, and even when they did it was often agreed that the natural leaders were the best men to entrust with the decisions. There could be no more striking instance than the fact that even in the elections to the Virginia ratifying Convention for the Federal Constitution, many districts were content to elect their two leading men regardless of the fact that they were of opposite opinions on the Constitution, while eight delegates voted contrary to the wishes of their constituents without any apparent loss of popularity.

Early organisers of the Republican Party both noticed and made use of the leading factor of personal influence. "The elections in Virginia," Madison informed James Monroe, who was in Paris, "are over and in part known. The only two districts in which the election turned on *political* rather than *personal* considerations, where those in which Alexandria and Winchester stand." And it is significant that these were city, not country, districts. John Randolph, reporting Federalist successes eight years later, remarked that the elections had been governed by "personal and local, rather than political, considerations," which he repeated with emphasis to another correspondent.

The insistent tendency of Virginia society to form itself on lines of rank and eminence reappeared to determine the character of the House of Burgesses before the Revolution. On a close analysis, however, it would certainly prove that many of the men who got into the House of Burgesses were neither great planters nor men of any particular distinction. In 1758 one of Richard Henry Lee's correspondents told him of the election of two new burgesses because he "knew no better way to support the independence of the legislature and guard the liberty of the subject than by now and then shifting the representatives of the people, especially those who have neither natural or acquired parts to recommend them." But the elected gentry recognised their own upper class, to whom they accorded a respect and leadership in the all-important committee system of the House. Although the general elections of the eighteenth century often resulted in fairly extensive alterations in membership, they seldom unsettled the leaders. In 1756, for example, no fewer than forty-one new members came into a House numbering 105, but the leadership remained in much the same hands. The central pillar of this establishment was Speaker John Robinson, first elected to that office in 1735, and thereafter both Speaker and Treasurer till his death in 1766. It was the Speaker who made most of the appointments to committees and through whose good offices the great families exercised their traditional control of the legislative process. He was in this both their good servant and their representative.

The proceedings of the House were continuously dominated by a select few. Between 1720 and 1776, out of 630 who sat throughout that period, these few numbered only 110. Only some twenty members continually took a leading part in its activities, and most of the leaders were actually provided by three families—the Robinsons, the Randolphs, and the Lees.

It is likely that the incursion into Williamsburg of Patrick Henry, and the weaknesses exposed by the notorious scandal of John Robinson's estate, which revealed to the world the fact that many of the leading men of the province had relied on secret loans out of public funds, probably helped to loosen the system. Robinson's successor as Speaker, Peyton Randolph, offered committee assignments to more members than before; but even this may have been a manoeuvre rather than a gesture, for inner groups never have much difficulty in controlling large committees.

This Virginia leadership was regarded by its contemporaries— and particularly by its opponents—as an aristocracy. Supporters of Jefferson would call its principles "aristocratic", a term of opprobrium opposite but similar to "democratic" when used of good republican Whigs—who were not democrats. Such designations must be kept in a due proportion. The great Virginia landowners did not make large incomes out of rent rolls; the social and economic equivalent lay in their slaves. Their mansions would have served as gatehouses on the estates of European noblemen. They were in fact gentry. Virginia had its fair share of Squire Westerns; and the cultural distinctions of the Virginians of this class belong rather to the realm of historical piety than of probable fact. In areas of recent settlement any serious degree of educational depth was almost unattainable. Conditions in the Valley during the revolutionary period wer alarmingly primitive; when Jefferson and Madison tried to spread the gospel of their Republican Party they were dismayed by the limited circulation and reading of newspapers, which were almost unknown in the West and were very little read outside the Tidewater and the towns. Yet even in the Valley the social tendency was in the same direction: nearly all the Valley's political leaders in the Revolution were themselves the proprietors of the larger estates. Representation in Virginia was a process of social selection. It was in fact the American version of the very unpopular theory of virtual representation. . . .

But an upper class is defined, realistically, in relation to its subordinates. The system which the county magnates of Virginia built up in the generation after Bacon's Rebellion was not a tightly closed one. The ordinary voter stood much closer to his representative in Virginia than he was likely to do in England; it was easier for men of ability, such as Edmund Pendleton, to rise through the ranks—though Pendleton had the patronage of a great family. A process of appraisal and selection of prudent recruitment from the ranks, was conducted by the local magnates in their own counties.

In the Federalist era, for perhaps ten years, political parties and national issues intruded into Virginia politics. A two-party system hardly took root in the state; but the party contest helped to splinter the fences of the old regime. It encroached on the personal character of the relationship between representative and electors by introducing considerations of general and impersonal policy.

The aims of parties encroached not only on the former privacy of the relationship between electors and representatives but, in a subtle way, on the tradition against campaign promises. If a candidate could be called on—even instructed—to throw his vote and influence on certain prescribed lines, it might be argued that, by agreeing or offering to do so, he was making a corrupt promise. The tension between the older ideas and newer needs was exposed in an interesting letter from the citizens of Norfolk to their state representative, Littleton W. Tazewell, later to be a leading figure in Virginian politics. "We hope never to see the day," they began, "when the principle of representation, the soul of our republic, shall be abused, polluted, and corrupted by the adoption of those electioneering arts which give the brazen and hollow sycophant the advantage over the man of modesty, virtue and talents. . . ." He had, therefore, a right to abstain from canvassing; but they on their side had a right to get his answer to several very pointed questions about his principles, which were suspected of being Federalist, and about his recent conduct in public office.

But in the domestic politics of Virginia, and in the heyday of the undivided leadership of the gentry, the question seldom arose, for the simple reason that few counties would have had the effrontery to instruct their leading citizens in their legislative duties. Instruction was hardly compatible with deference.

PART TWO
Parties and the Maria Theresa Syndrome

Political parties arose out of the welter of interests and opinions that marked the new, national republic after 1789. In effect, the process began with the establishment of the Constitution in that year. A common, functioning political arena is another prerequisite for party formation; and the character of the arena will have profound effects on parties. For the first time, the new Constitution created a truly national arena.

The initial stirrings of party formation appeared at the national capital, briefly in New York and then at Philadelphia until 1800. When Alexander Hamilton began to forge connections with members of George Washington's cabinet and with men in Congress, he was not consciously trying to build a party. Indeed, he would have hotly denied that he was doing so. He was, as he saw it, only trying to bring some coherence into affairs in order to promote his broad conception of national economic development, and to serve various interests that he favored. Before he was finished, however, he and his cohorts had launched the first national political party. Opposition inevitably emerged, led at first by James Madison in the House of Representatives and later by Thomas Jefferson, Albert Gallatin of Pennsylvania, and others. An increasingly sharp conflict over issues of foreign policy divided men further as they watched the course of the French Revolutionary wars and took sides as "Anglomen" or "Gallomen." Hamiltonians plumped for monarchical England, and Jeffersonians for republican France. Acrimonious controversy over the Jay Treaty with England in 1795 brought the initial stage of party formation to virtual completion.

In the process, leaders at the capital reached out into the countryside for support and sought to mobilize stable followings behind them. These local formations, as William Nisbet Chambers observes, were assembled by local party workers in the states, and in the counties and towns. One result was that party structures became deeper and broader than most early factions had been—more dense in the number and variety of individuals, groups, and interests they embraced. They were also more complex or highly-articulated in their working structures than factions usually were; and they were generally more stable or durable. Finally, parties took on distinctive senses of internal identity, of "we" versus "they," of Federalists against Republicans, each with their own ideology. Indeed, ideological contention proved to be a central, catalytic agent in the creation of the first parties.

Events soon brought party development to a second and more advanced stage. The national elections of 1796 were fought in a party spirit, as were many local contests. The crucial election that made Jefferson President in 1800 raised party activity to new levels, and his first term brought the Republicans to a peak of patisan action. Meanwhile candidates for office assumed new, partisan visibility and, indeed, responsibility. Voting on policy questions in Congress revealed an increasingly consistent, partisan character as most Federalists or Republicans voted together on opposite sides. Generally voters could know, if they took the trouble, about where the men they elected to office would stand. The result was relatively effective and responsive representation, and a reasonably clear choice of alternatives for the voter. The Federalists never quite became a wholly modern, full-scale political party; they appeared, instead, as a kind of transitional formation. The Republican phalanx, however, ultimately emerged as a distinctively modern, popular party despite its infusion of elite leadership and older political styles.

Against this background, another precondition for party formation may be discerned. This condition was a relatively high level of heterogeneity in society or social structure which, in turn, produced a complex variety of conflicting interests and attitudes. In the far-flung new nation as a whole—and within a few economically advanced and variegated states themselves—such variety abounded. Party architects had to work with these materials, had to represent varied interests, and had to reconcile competing groups as best they could, if they were to win power and to manage public affairs. This variety made the job of assembling party structures intricate and difficult. Yet it also provided an impetus for political formations that could bring differing interests under one roof, and could offer some sort of unifying point of view or ideology. The final step was a sense of felt need among working politicians for these structures, and the skill to do the job. The first party system was the result.

That system was more oriented to substantive policy issues than most American parties have been; and party contention reached threatening proportions. The "crisis points" are systematically delineated by the late Morton Grodzins, from Hamilton's funding plans and the Whiskey Rebellion of 1794 to the Alien and Sedition Acts and other confrontations. Much of the domestic conflict was precipitated by issues of world politics, including America's first "undeclared war" (with France); and in the Fries Uprising of 1799, a protest against war measures took the form of armed rebellion. War issues also brought on the first instances of significant, national intraparty factionalism. As President John Adams turned to a moderate course and sought peace, Hamilton and other "High Federalists" pressed for a more aggressive, warlike policy. One result was a sharp reversal for the Federalists at the polls.

Even as party rivalry reached its peak, as Richard Hofstadter observes, men like Adams and Jefferson "had no use for political parties"—in theory, although not in practice. Indeed, there was little in the political culture Americans inherited from England or from their colonial experience to sustain a favorable view of parties. The very word, "party," was closely identified with "faction"; and factious activity was by definition evil and disruptive. The men who wrought the Federalist and Republican parties worked in the face of this "anti-party cant." Yet they were struggling against themselves as well as against their opponents, although it was usually the *other* party, or party *conflict*, that they professed to abhor. Partisans declaiming against parties as they went on making parties: one is reminded of Frederick the Great's estimate of Maria Theresa's role in the partition of Poland. "She weeps," he quipped, "but she keeps on taking." Parties were built, but it was years before profession would catch up with practice.

In the face of anti-party attitudes, ordinary citizens as well as leaders were nonetheless taking on partisan connections. These loyalties were seldom so strong as they would become later, especially in the Golden Age of parties from the 1830s to the 1890s. In a study of the last phase of the Federalist party, however, David Hackett Fischer has provided a revealing analysis of the kind of men who inclined to one party or the other. The endeavor is a difficult one: voting data for the period is hard to come by, and analysis must depend, in part, on scattered and impressionistic evidence. In one aspect, it was a matter of geography. Grossly by section, New England was heavily Federalist and the South was mostly Republican. Thus, the main competitive ground lay in the swing states of New York, Pennsylvania, and (later) Maryland and New Jersey. At a deeper level, the division appeared to fall along lines of what today we might call Establishment (generally Federalist) or anti-Establishment (generally Republican), although the older, English usage of the term might be more appropriate to the divisions of the time; and in Virginia, at least, Republicans were about as established as Federalists were. The kinds of communities men lived in were also relevant. Towns or counties that were growing, gaining in population, "on the make," tended to be Republican; more staid, settled, homogeneous, less dynamic areas that showed little or no gain in population tended to be Federalist. Add to these and other features a variety of ethnic and religious ties of the sort that have affected political preferences throughout the American experience, and the picture is complex indeed.

The forces that shaped the first American party system were intricate. But they make for a far more interesting story than the accounts of earlier historians would suggest.

FROM NATIONAL FACTION
TO NATIONAL PARTY

5   FROM   *William Nisbet Chambers*
Party Development and Party Action

With only one [partial] exception, early American state politics
was non-party politics. This was true. . .even in the contest (or
contests) over ratification [of the Constitution] in 1787, and it
remained true in the initial "national" elections for President and
Congress in 1788-1789, when for the first time a potential national
electoral arena existed. In the states themselves, politics was a
kaleidescopic flux of interest groupings and opinion aggregates, of
free-style individual action, of shifting alignments between notable-leaders, groups, unstable factions, juntos, caucuses, and
cliques.

SOURCE. William Nisbet Chambers, "Party Development and Party Action: the
American Origins," pp. 95-106. Copyright c 1963 by Wesleyan University. Re-
printed from *History and Theory,* Volume III, Number 1, by permission of Wesleyan
University Press, publisher.

The configurations of the political hurly-burly varied from state to state. So also. . .did the methods of politics, whether in nominations, elections, legislative behavior, or propaganda. Only sophisticated Pennsylvania, with its continuing rivalry between organized Constitutionalists and Republicans (the titles referred to state issues) brewed [something like] a state party system. Yet even in Pennsylvania the alignments of leaders and interests between and within the parties were often nearly invisible to any but the practiced eye. In New York, sometimes marked as a state with parties, politics actually continued with the old gruel of personal-family cliques and satellite factions. . . .Methods were sophisticated enough to foreshadow Tammany Hall, but principals like George Clinton or agents like Alexander Hamilton remained the foci of political formations. These formations showed many similarities to the old Whig "connexions" of eighteenth-century England, depending as they did on the leadership and patronage of notables, important personages, or magnates, and resting as they did on intricate webs of personal ties. Indeed, Edmund Burke would have found them familiar.

Despite variations. . .this early American state politics may be described most generally as *faction politics*—with the variations lying in personal cliques, the planter-elite "Fifty Families" junto in Maryland, the caucuses of Massachusetts, and the like.

Analysis of these early formations affords some important distinctions. Generally, a *faction* appeared as a portion of an electorate, political elite, or legislature, whose adherents were engaged in parallel action or co-ordination of some consistency but of limited durability, in conflict with other portions. Innumerable such loose factions characterized the early American scene. A *clique* was a portion whose relationships depended upon a commanding individual, a family, or a close coterie of personal associates; generally, the death or retirement of the focal individual led to the extinction of the clique. A junto, as the term was commonly used, meant a portion which operated as a small, often secret, dominant group at a seat of government, whether state, county, or town; this variety of formation was most commonly found in the Southern states. A *caucus* was generally the coordinating nucleus group of a larger faction. None of these formations took on the stature of a party, and such formations were not generally thought of as parties by contemporaries. It is in this sense of its hinging on factions rather than parties that we may speak of early American politics as "faction politics," using the term "faction" to include lesser but similar formations such as cliques, juntos, and caucuses. Except where factions were unusually broad in their range, we might speak of "connexion politics." It is with such patterns of political operation, and their implications, that we shall later contrast party politics.

Faction politics in America in the 1770s and 1780s was, broadly speaking, premodern. Like English politics in the eighteenth century, it depended heavily on personalities and personal connections, and often on the deference of plain men to "notabilistic" leaders. Again like English politics, it was disorderly, subject to abrupt changes, and semi-invisible—often, for example, the factional ties of candidates or government officials were unknown to the public, or changed without notice from election to election or between elections; and few factions showed much durability. While political methods were frequently sophisticated, they were also highly variable and subject to change according to the impulses of leaders of the moment. Policy-making was, like much policy-making in eighteenth-century England, heavily influenced by shifting factional or bloc combinations in the legislatures, by clique or junto domination, by the plurality of group pressures or opinions at the moment, and by individual caprice. In short, early American faction politics lacked the degrees of order, visible continuity and relative clarity of political formations or positions, and stable rationalization of political methods, which may be counted among the characteristics of modern party politics. Compared with English politics of the same era, however, it was less hierarchical, aristocratic, or elitist, and in this sense may be viewed as a transitional form.

Such politics also offered differential advantages to persons or groups who stood high on the scale of property, position, and power. Government was broadly republican and a substantial potential electorate existed despite property and tax qualifications. The extreme looseness, semi-invisibility, and confusion of informal politics, however, tended to limit effective popular influence, to the advantage of "well-placed" interests.

Although the Constitution of 1787 provided a national electoral arena, obstacles to the formation of national parties remained. The pluralism of American society and early politics—regional dissimilarities, the variety of economic undertakings, the multiplicity of groups and religious sects, varying perspectives across the country—all stood in the way. Individuals resisted being herded, many citizens feared what George Washington called "the baneful effects of the spirit of party generally," and state leaders and populations clung to special local identities and interests against national "consolidation."

The earliest impetus for party formation came from the new center of national government. Furthermore, as Joseph Charles has argued effectively, party origins sprang from cleavage over significant national issues affecting the shape the new nation would take, and over general ideological outlooks, together with critical questions of world politics and foreign policy. Controversies which began at the national capital were carried to the country, and provided the reference points for party development.

The first representative leader in polarizing proto-party forces was Hamilton, whose political style is thus critically relevant. In a new, almost unstructured situtation, he stepped forward as a bold advocate determined to create policy innovation, and his controversial five-point program for capitalist development was far more than a mere reflex to established views of business interest groups. To innovation Hamilton added a driving, shrewd talent for political management—in the executive branch, in the Senate and House of Representatives, in caucuses, with notable-leaders across the country, and with the public. The effects of Hamilton's initial leadership told first on Congressional behavior. From his post as President Washington's Secretary of the Treasury, he worked to establish ties between the separated executive and legislative branches. In doing so, he gathered an entourage of sympathizers in the cabinet and of caucusing followers in Congress, who came soon to constitute a distinct capital faction. In the process he was able to rely on the prestige of Washington's name and generally on Washington's support. By the sessions of 1790 and 1791, the scattered and individualistic activity that had marked the first session in 1789 began to show signs of co-ordination and policy coherence.

Before long, Hamilton's leadership (and politics in general) also became embroiled in world issues. The French Revolution was at first widely hailed in America/but regicide, the rise of the Jacobins, radical republicanism, and the Terror, followed by France's declaration of war on Great Britain in February, 1793, divided Americans sharply. A lush pamphlet and periodical literature sprang up. Men took sides emotionally as Anglomen (stigmatized by opponents as "Monocrats") or Gallomen (stigmatized in turn as "Jacobins"). Thus issues of domestic interests and outlook were supplemented by ideological reactions to European events and the result was a further consolidation of political forces.

In time, a series of steps led from the Hamiltonian capital *faction* to a national Federalist *party.* The process may be summarized under four headings.

First, linkages of association, parallel action, and finally coordination were extended from the capital into the states, counties, and towns. Correspondents, personal friends, natural sympathizers, business associates, the many individuals whom Hamilton as Secretary of the Treasury had been able to oblige—all were sounded. Active response came particularly from local notables such as former military officers, mercantile magnates in New York, Congregational divines in New England, and many planter-nabobs in the South. National leaders gave cues to local leaders and to lesser party spokesmen and sponsors in the localities, and such men came to form the working vertebrae of the party. Many of them stood as prototypes of a new breed of party politicians, or party "cadre". In short, a firm and distinctive Federalist structure was in the process of forming and of finding a following.

Second, national leaders and local leaders or cadre collaborated to develop increasingly standardized ways of performing certain key political functions. These ranged from managing and connecting (between branches) in government, to nominating candidates, electioneering and mobilizing voters, and shaping opinion in the states and localities. A national factional or party paper under John Fenno, the *Gazette of the United States,* disseminated Federalist perspectives, and local sheets followed its lead.

Third, a substantial combination of interests and opinions was enlisted in the Federalist following [including]. . .many wage-earners, particularly in shipbuilding, and farmers producing commercial and particularly export crops/and thus, contrary to the conception of much of the older historiography, the Federalists possessed a significant mass base—although their Achilles heel remained an insensitivity to the concerns of agriculture as a whole. The interests of all these groups were not necessarily identical, however, and Hamilton and other leaders in developing policy inevitably performed a function of political brokerage, devising at least tacit formulas of agreement among the varied groups.

In time, a series of steps led from the Hamiltonian capital *faction* to a national Federalist *party*. The process may be summarized under four headings.

First, linkages of association, parallel action, and finally co-ordination were extended from the capital into the states, counties, and towns. Correspondents, personal friends, natural sympathizers, business associates, the many individuals whom Hamilton as Secretary of the Treasury had been able to oblige—all were sounded. Active response came particularly from local notables such as former military officers, mercantile magnates in New York, Congregational divines in New England, and many planter-nabobs in the South. National leaders gave cues to local leaders and to lesser party spokesmen and sponsors in the localities, and such men came to form the working vertebrae of the party. Many of them stood as prototypes of a new breed of party politicians, or party "cadre". In short, a firm and distinctive Federalist structure was in the process of forming and of finding a following.

Second, national leaders and local leaders or cadre collaborated to develop increasingly standardized ways of performing (between branches) in government, to nominating candidates, electioneering and mobilizing voters, and shaping opinion in the states and localities. A national factional or party paper under John Fenno, the *Gazette of the United States*, disseminated Federalist perspectives, and local sheets followed its lead.

Third, a substantial combination of interests and opinions was enlisted in the Federalist following [including]. . .many wage-earners, particularly in shipbuilding, and farmers producing commercial and particularly export crops; and thus, contrary to the conception of much of the older historiography, the Federalists possessed a significant mass base—although their Achilles heel remained an insensitivity to the concerns of agriculture as a whole.

The interests of all these groups were not necessarily identical, however, and Hamilton and other leaders in developing policy inevitably performed a function of political brokerage, devising at least tacit formulas of agreement among the varied groups.

Fourth, the emerging Federalist force developed distinctive attitudes and unifying faiths and loyalties—in short, the beginnings of a partisan ideology. At the outset, the charisma of Washington was a key ingredient, and Hamilton remarked years later that "he [Washington] was an *Aegis very essential to me*". Other items became integral to the Federalists persuasion, such as a stress on "respectability," a concern for national capitalist growth and stability, an emphasis on a national government which was strong and "energetic," an elitist tone. In the backwash of revolutionary Jacobinism, Federalists also saw themselves as a bulwark against a threatening world-revolutionary spirit, of sanity against madness, of order against chaos. Thus ties of interest were supplemented by shared outlooks and symbolism. Indeed, it was the development of the emotional *elan* of ideology, more than any other element, which marked the transition of the Federalists from faction to party.

The upshot of all these developments was a new kind of national linkage. It was far more than a "connexion," in the old sense of a shifting set of personal, familial, or clique relationships. It was rather a stable "connection," in the modern spelling and meaning, a structure of men across the nation who not only shared interests, but who were coming together into co-ordinated rationalized patterns of action around a set of national leaders, on the basis of shared social, economic, political, or moral perspectives. It was, or became by sometime around 1793 or 1794, a. . .party in the proper sense. . . .

Two observations may be made concerning this development. First, although the Federalist party was in part a combination of groups, it was also *more* than a combination of groups. . .in that it was an articulated, semi-independent structure of stable relationships between leaders, cadre, and following, built by the purposeful energies of men, who gave it more in action than they took in reflex reaction to group impulses. Second, the party did not exhibit any significant degree of organizations in the strict sense. If we insist on seeing party as organization [in the twentieth-century sense] we will have very little to say about America's first national party.

Opposition to the Federalists was soon forthcoming. It also took form at the capital, where James Madison in the House of Representatives played initial antagonist to Hamilton's protagonist—contrary again to much of the conventional historiography, which lists Jefferson as the founder of the Republican party. From the outset, however, the Republican opposition moved in accord with popular stirrings of interest and opinion.

Dissent in the states, counties, and towns was directed at Hamilton's economic program, but it also turned to issues of foreign policy and world-political ideology. After Washington's proclamation of neutrality towards warring France and England in 1793, for example, an opposition voice in the western reaches of Pennsylvania cried out that "the cause of France is the cause of man, and neutrality is desertion." In 1794 John Taylor of Virginia published a fat polemical pamphlet, *A Definition of Parties, or the Political Effects of the Paper System Considered*, which gave focus to the domestic and world-political strains of opposition. In 1795 widespread protest against the treaty the Federalist John Jay had negotiated with Great Britain drew divisions over issues of world politics even more sharply. Meanwhile, gaining momentum in 1793 and 1794, several local political associations had sprung up across the country. Called variously Democratic or Republican Societies, they were remarkable for the number of intellectuals in their memebership and leadership though, as Eugene Link has shown, they drew on a number of elements in the population. They were also remarkably modern, in that they were open, voluntary assemblages of individual men, and in the degree of formal organization they achieved under democratically adopted constitutions, Their approach originally was largely in terms of ideology, discussion of political philosophy and issues, and propaganda; but they also doled out blessings or censure on members of Congress and endorsed candidates for elections. They began to disappear after Washington, in the wake of the Whisky Insurrection of 1794, denounced them as "self-created societies," presumably all disruptive of public order. Yet, flourishing as they did from Vermont to South Carolina and Kentucky, they were significant while they lasted. The varievoices of dissent and their

institutionalization in the Societies indicate the degree to which
the Republican opposition was indigenous in nature, and of local
and popular origin, rather than simply a product of mobilization
by leaders at the center of government. Such coruscations did not,
however, make a party. Rather, they constituted a potential
following for a potential party.

The Republican party found its structure in linkages between
the Congressional faction Madison was drawing together at the
capital and the groundwork of national opposition. No bold,
creative antagonist, Madison began slowly though industriously in
the session of 1790 and moved painfully ahead in succeeding
sessions, relying particularly on the Virginia men and increasingly
on certain members from Pennsylvania. In particular John Beckley
of Virginia, Clerk of the House, worked behind the scenes and
began to exhibit talents as a national cadre politician that would
have been admired by later Van Burens, Hannas, Cannons, or
Farleys. From their base in Congress, Republican leaders reached
out to the countryside. Like the Federalists before them, they
gradually established connections in states and localities; encouraged the development of local leaders and cadre; labored to co-
ordinate the choice of candidates, election activites, and propaganda; secured a general following; and worked up a significant
group combination. National leaders made fruitful connections
with the Clintonians in New York and with remnants of the old
state-Constitutionalists in Pennsylvania, but elsewhere their local
elements were generally newly built. With the founding of the
National Gazette under the poet-polemicist Philip Freneau in 1791,
and an alignment of satellite papers, they established a loose
information office which gave impetus to distinctively Republican
attitudes and *elan*.

The Republican forces were slower in effecting a clearly party-
like structure than the Federalists, however—and again, it was an
issue with intensely emotional, symbolic, and ideological overtones
that brought them to full party status. It is probably not proper to
speak of a stable Republican *party* nationally earlier than the Jay
Treaty controversy of 1795 and Congressional debate of 1796, the
assumption by Jefferson of effective party leadership in the latter
year, and the intensification of cleavages in political perspectives
which contention over the treaty engendered.

As they shaped a party formation, the Republicans exhibited distinctive characteristics in their general attitude toward relations between leaders and followers, and in the character of their party structure. Unlike the tone of the Federalists, which was broadly elitist, the tone of the Republicans was broadly democratic. To Federalist leaders, the purposes of party were to amass and stabilize support in the public and electorate for policies the leaders had already adopted. Their party was overwhelmingly a "party of notables," in [Max] Weber's term, despite their significant mass base. Republican leaders, who were in effect evolving a formation which marked a transitional stage between a "party of notables" and a "party of politicians," generally believed that the relationship between leaders and mass following should include responsiveness or responsibility to the wishes and opinions of the following, and that policy should in some degree be shaped accordingly. Thus the Republican ideology embraced a considerable notion of intra-party democracy, in which party following might play a somewhat less "passive" and more "active" role than Weber's abstract formulation suggests. The matter is put aptly if too simply by [E.E.] Robinson, when he speaks of Federalists approaching elections as merely "a test upon [their] policies," while Republicans, viewed elections as "a guide to the desires of public opinion." In short, we may conceptualize the Federalists as operating in terms of *plebiscitarian* ideology and action, while the Republicans moved in terms of *democratic* ideology and action. It is thus possible to speak of the Republicans not only as a modern party, but as a "*popular*" party, in the sense of a party grounded in and sensitive to a broad and durable base in the population of electorate. Despite recurring counter-tendencies to oligarchy noted by [Robert] Michels, this is the form that many modern parties have taken in nation after nation in the last century and a half. Others, however, have pursued the plebiscitarian path.

Furthermore, as compared with the Federalists, Republican development was not only more popular but more complex. The indigenous opposition movement developed sometimes ahead of, and at least partially independently of, the Madisonian capital faction. This was notably the case with the Democratic or Republican Societies. Some writers have leapt to the conclusion that these associations were integral, organized local units in a national Republican party; actually, however, there was no structural connection between the Madisonian capital faction on the one hand and the Societies on the other. Rather, as Noble E. Cunningham argues persuasively, the associations acted as pressure groups, with a primarily ideological approach. The significance of indigenous Republican sentiment and the Democratic-Republican groups is that they provided pre-existing enclaves of support at the periphery to which Madisonians at the center could reach out. Contrary to [Maurice] Duverger's suggestion that parties of the "cadre" type are typically generated from the center "out," as the Federalists were, they may also emerge in part from the periphery "in," as the Republicans did, in a very complex pattern indeed.

Finally, the Republican party came to include some organization in the strict sense, as a continuing rationalized division of labor and co-ordination of functions toward shared goals. Indeed, figures like Beckley and Freneau or his press-successor Benjamin Franklin Bache show an obvious kinship with Disraeli's later Taper or Tadpole, who tied up votes or swam in the muddy waters of opinion in Great Britain in the 1830s and 1840s. Organization was spotty, however, and its full development remains a phenomenon of later mature parties of politicians with an enlarged mass electorate to mobilize.

In the development of both the Federalist and the Republican parties, ideology played a catalytic role. As it appeared in this development, it was partial rather than total, consistent with a basic national consensus, and somewhat amorphous—though not so loose as the flaccid ideological outlooks of later American parties have often become. . . .Yet a sense of identity and direction, patterns of commitment, at least a loose world-view, what Washington called "the spirit of party generally," and consequent cohesion and *elan*, were all essential ingredients in the consolidation of durable linkages of Federalist and Republican party structure and action, and all may be thought of as ideological components. Ideology as it appeared in American party development, furthermore, was more than merely a rationalization of interests, a shadowy variable dependent on economic or other self-oriented group concerns, or a figment of the psyche to satisfy inward personal needs. It was rather a positive force which shaped perceptions (or misperceptions) of political reality. It thereby generated faiths and loyalties which might have remained dormant, and prompted effective political action.

The establishment of parties brought a significant degree of order to American politics. Parties operated as continuing bonds between the decision-making processes of government on the one hand, and individuals and groups in the public and electorate on the other. Distinguishable party positions were put forth, and Congressional behavior was increasingly bipolarized on partisan lines at the expense of dwindling numbers of center-individualists. Candidates for office ran as Federalists or Republicans, thereby providing voters with a reasonably clear two-way choice. More and more voters identified with party symbols and party ideology. Thus, in the emergence of two-party politics and rivalry, pluralism was harnessed to some degree, the effects of state-by-state fragmentation in politics were reduced, and political methods were increasingly rationalized, standardized, and modernized.

Party politics also reduced the differential advantages in power that had fallen to well-placed individuals and groups. Farmers, small traders, artisans, members of low-status religious groups, many intellectuals, reformers, even aliens found in the Jeffersonian Republican party a representative of their interests, perspectives, opinions, and rights, as against the demands of larger property, ascribed position, high respectability, and established influence. The existence of the two parties in competition provided a meaningful option between Federalist and Republican perspectives, policies, and leaders; and voters quickly learned to make use of the choice the parties put before them. Thus, in an open political system, the first modern political parties brought such important gains in democracy as representation, substantial participation, and choice. In a few short years, the new American nation—decades before its british ancestors—had moved well into a new world-era of politics.

POLITICAL PARTIES AND ISSUES TO 1800

6   FROM   *Morton Grodzins*
           Parties and the Crisis of Succession

The first American parties became visible before the end of Washington's [presidential] term. Any brief statement of the doctrinal differences between the two groups—one of which became known as the Federalists, the other as Anti-Federalists, Jeffersonians, or Republicans—inevitably effaces important nuances. . . .

From the founding of the new United States in 1789 until 1800 the government was firmly in control of the Federalists, whose leader was Alexander Hamilton. Federalist policies were based on

SOURCE. Selections from Morton Grodzins, "Political Parties and the Crisis of Succession in the United States: The Case of 1800," in *Political Parties and Political Development,* ed. Joseph LaPalombara and Myron Weiner (copyright c 1966 by Princeton University Press; Princeton Paperback, 1968). Reprinted by permission of Princeton University Press.

Hamilton's view that governments had to be ruled by gentlemen, by his distrust of popular majorities, and by his conviction that American progress depended upon bringing the wealthy and well-born to the firm support of the new government. Since during this period farm population ranged from 90 to 95 per cent of the total, Hamilton's party was not exclusively a party of merchants and traders. If it had been, whatever the existing limitations on suffrage, the party could not have maintained itself in office. Nevertheless the principal points of the Federalist program were aimed at promoting the interests of urban mercantile groups and fostering the development of business and industry. The great Hamiltonian measures of the first years of the republic included the funding and assumption of the revolutionary debts (funding paid off the sharply depreciated debts of the old confederation at their face value; assumption made the federal government respon-sible for state debts, which were even more depressed). Both policies, and especially assumption, gave enormous profits to speculators who had purchased state securities from their original holders at a fraction of their face value. A protective tariff (the first bill introduced into the first Congress), the establishment of the first United States bank, excise taxes on whiskey, sale of public lands in large tracts, and a strongly pro-English foreign policy were all a part of the Hamiltonian program; and all of them were designed "to bind the moneyed classes firmly to the central government."

Controversy over early Federalist policies was blunted because they were carried out under the presidency of the respected hero of the Revolution, George Washington, who (like a more recent general-president) was largely dependent upon staff work and staff recommendations. Washington, said Hamilton, was an "aegis very essential" for his purposes. . . .As Washington increasingly al-lowed Hamilton to dominate the policies of the administration, so Jefferson increasingly grew restive in his cabinet position where he found himself "daily pitted [against Hamilton] in the cabinet like two cocks."

The first scratches of disagreement soon developed into wounds, and the period from 1794 to 1800 seemed to those who lived through it, as it now seems to afterviewers, one in which a growing crescendo of political discord threatened the very existence of the nation. Federalists and Republicans divided on each successive issue. Here, in brief review, are the most important crisis points:

Whiskey Rebellion. In 1794 farmers of Western Pennsylvania and neighboring sections of Virginia took up arms against the federal tax on distilled liquors. Whiskey to those who made it was not the luxury that Hamilton conceived it to be but a basic commodity, more potable and portable than corn, and a medium of exchange on the frontier. The rebellious group had the sympathy of many farmers and tradesmen throughout the country (people who were beginning to think of themselves as Republicans) though Republican leaders had little sympathy with the tactic of armed insurrection. Washington dispatched no fewer than 13,000 troops to the scene (Hamilton accompanied them), and the rebellion collapsed. Jefferson viewed the sequence of events as a gloomy augury that the nation might be breaking up.

The Jay Treaty. Debate over ratification of the Jay Treaty (1795) brought about a deeper and more general division of the nation. The movement of the French Revolution from moderation to violence (and the war between France and Great Britain which began in February 1793) had already separated pro-British Federalists from pro-French Republicans. Washington's course of official neutrality was viewed by Republican leaders as a retreat from the revolutionary spirit of 1776 and, more specifically, as a betrayal of treaties with France that dated back to this nation's period of greatest need. The French-British war produced tensions between each of the combatant nations and the United States. John Jay's mission to London was aimed at reducing these tensions with Great Britain (for example, the harassment of our shipping and impressment of our sailors) as well as at solving long-standing issues between the two nations (for example, the incitement of Indians in American territory by the British in Canada). Even many Federalists, and Washington among them, were unhappy with the treaty as it was finally negotiated. Washington kept the text of the treaty for four months before submitting it to the Senate. It was debated and passed by the Senate in secret session, but the text soon leaked to the Republican press, which immediately launched a campaign of criticism. Republicans organized petitions, issued pamphlets against ratification, hanged Jay in effigy, and stoned Hamilton in the streets of New York.

Federalists denounced those who took part in the criticism as "the scum of the society." The national debate was prolonged as Washington hesitated over signing the treaty and, subsequently, as the House of Representatives debated at length an appropriation that was necessary to effectuate it. The appropriation carried only under Federalist threats that a failure to do so would cause the dissolution of the country or war with Great Britain. Jefferson regarded the treaty as a betrayal of the Revolution; Federalists responded that the only opposition to the treaty came from those who were the tools of France. Washington admitted that the public mind was agitated over the Jay Treaty "in a higher degree than it has been at any period since the Revolution."

XYZ Affair. If the nascent Republican party gained strength because of popular disapproval of the Jay Treaty, the advantage was all to the Federalists in the XYZ affair of 1798. The five years between the Jay Treaty and the XYZ affair were years of internal political turmoil and steadily worsening relations with France. John Adams replaced Washington as President in 1796, Thomas Jefferson, the leader of the opposition, being selected Vice President as the consequence of disagreement in Federalist ranks and a quirk of the election laws. Even during the election the French minister to the United States openly campaigned for Jefferson and hinted at war between France and the United States if Jefferson were not elected. And from the first day of his administration Adams was caught up in difficulties with France. The Directory refused in an insulting manner to recognize Adams' new diplomatic representative to France, Charles C. Pinckney (brother of Adams' running mate, Thomas Pinckney). An undeclared war at sea broke out between France and the United States. Adams at every turn of affairs was faced by demands from Hamilton, Secretary of State Timothy Pickering, and other High Federalists for an all-out war against France. Instead, Adams asked for and received congressional authorization to increase the size of the army and navy (against Republican opposition). At the same time he dispatched John Marshall and Elbridge Gerry to join Pinckney in Paris for a new round of negotiations in search of an agreement that would lead to peace and commercial treaty. The French government avoided the new envoys for weeks. Finally they were approached by three unofficial agents of the Directory who demanded, as a prerequisite to negotiations, an American loan to France as well as bribes to certain French officials. The Americans refused, and negotiations were broken off. When the correspondence between the negotiators was laid before Congress in the spring of 1798 (Adams substituted the letters X, Y, and Z for the names of the French emissaries), congressional and popular indignation ran high.

The XYZ affair catapulted Adams to a high point of popularity. Republicans, including Jefferson, who still served as Vice President, were condemned as actual or near traitors, "Frenchmen in all their feelings and wishes." High Federalists went so far as to charge Republicans with being ready to join an invading French army on American beachheads. Hamilton and others were confident that the XYZ affair would "give a most fatal blow to the Jacobins." And Republican opposition was nearly nonexistent as Congress authorized new efforts to strengthen the army, fortify harbors, and build new ships. Jeffersonians speculated that the nation's new military might would be turned against them.

The Alien and Sedition Laws. The XYZ affair allowed Federalists to identify Republicans with France and thus to consider opposition to administration measures as seditious or traitorous. France became the external, Republicans the internal, foe. With national defense and political orthodoxy their main planks, Federalists worked to perpetuate themselves in power. "Under the guise of patriotic purpose and internal security, [they] enacted a program to cripple, if not destroy, the Jeffersonian party."

The Federalists' principal instruments were four laws passed during the spring and summer of 1798, the Alien and Sedition Acts. Three of the laws were aimed at aliens. (Many Republican converts and pamphleteers were relatively recent arrivals to the United States from Great Britain, Ireland, and France.) The period required for admission to citizenship was increased from five to fourteen years. The President was authorized to deport any alien deemed "dangerous to the peace and safety of the United States," and a failure to obey such a deportation order was punishable by imprisonment. Enemy aliens were subject to summary restraint and removal. The Sedition Act itself was aimed at all residents of the country, not just aliens. It provided heavy criminal penalties for the writing, printing, or speaking of "any false, scandalous, and malicious" words which were judged by a federal court to bring the government, President, or Congress "into contempt or disrepute."

The Alien Laws had the effect of silencing noncitizens and of encouraging the emigration of many, but President Adams was not aggresive in the use of his deportation powers. Though warrants for the seizure of several aliens were signed by the President, not a single alien was deported under the acts. The case was altogether different for the Sedition Law. The foremost historian of the Sedition Act [James M. Smith] has verified seventeen indictments taken under it (plus three others that were inspired by the act but were returned under the common law). In addition, a number of arrests were made that were not followed by formal indictments. The principal thrust of the prosecutions was against the proprietors, editors, and chief writers of Republican newspapers. Of the five most influential Jeffersonian journals in the country (the Philadelphia *Aurora,* the Boston *Independent Chronicle,* the New York *Argus,* the Richmond *Examiner,* and the Baltimore *American*), only the last escaped a suit. Minor Republican newspapers were not ignored, and several were forced to cease publication. A number of political leaders, including at least one congressman, were prosecuted. . . .

The Virginia and Kentucky Resolutions. . . .

The most important Republican response to the Alien and Sedition Laws were the Virginia and Kentucky Resolutions, drafted by Madison and Jefferson and passed by the legislatures of the two states. Each resolution condemned the Sedition Act and its companion measures on the grounds that they were unlawful exercises of national power. Though steering clear of proposals for secession, the resolutions declared that the states were the rightful judges of the limits of the central government's power. Since the Alien and Sedition Laws exceeded the delegated powers of the central government, those laws (to quote the Kentucky statement) were "void and of no force." It was the duty of the states "to interpose for arresting the progress of the evil." The Virginia legislature added action to words and ordered the state to reorganize and increase its militia and levy taxes for munitions. A number of Federalists took the resolutions to be portent of civil war. Hamilton himself suggested that Virginia be put "to the test of resistance," and that with regular troops (as opposed to the militia) he would not hesitate "to subdue a refractory and powerful State."

Fries' Rebellion. Subsequent events deprived Hamilton of the opportunity to subdue a state. But for the second time in five years military forces were needed in 1799 to put down an armed rebellion against Federalist policies. In the wake of the XYZ affair Congress was spurred on by High Federalists, seeking an official declaration of war with France, to increase military expenditures substantially. Such measures needed taxes to support them, and Congress levied a direct tax on dwelling houses, land, and slaves. . . .This resistance led to a number of arrests by the federal marshals, but the prisoners were rescued by an armed group under the leadership of John Fries. The insurgents marched about the countryside intimidating the assessors and gaining new recuits until Fries led a band of several hundred men. Federal troops were dispatched, and the rebellion immediately put down. Fries was captured and subsequently tried for treason.

* * *

The Federalist party became badly split during the period of national tension between 1794 and 1800. The conflict had its beginnings in Hamilton's defection from John Adams in the campaign of 1796. Nevertheless Adams carried over in his cabinet three High Federalists—the Secretaries of State (Timothy Pickering), Treasury (Oliver Wolcott), and War (James McHenry)—who were each in his own way more loyal to Hamilton than to the President. Hamilton also had great influence in both houses of Congress, and it was often difficult to tell whether the leadership of the country was being exercised by the President or the ex-Secretary of the Treasury. The principal plank of Hamilton's High Federalist policy was war with France and an alliance with Great Britain. The rigors of war, and, consequently, the military forces made available to the central government, would supply at once the occasion and the resources for sweeping away all Republican opposition, already "traitors" in Federalist eyes for their sympathy toward France.

Internal strains within Federalist ranks led finally to an open split in the party. While his cabinet and High Federalists in the Congress were calling for formal war with France (the informal war at sea was still being fought), President Adams was exploring the path to peace. Shortly after the XYZ papers had been sent to Congress Adams stated that he would not send a new minister to France without official assurance that the envoy would be "received, respected, and honored as the representative of a great, free powerful, and independent nation." When the French foreign minister, Talleyrand, gave assurances that these conditions would be met, Adams sent to the Senate (February 18, 1799) a nomination for a new envoy to Paris whose task would be to negotiate a peaceful settlement of French-American affairs. Adams did not even bother to consult with his cabinet, and the nomination "came as a bombshell to the cabinet and to the High Federalists." Adams went so far as to threaten to resign if the Senate did not approve the new mission to France—a threat the High Federalists would have welcomed if its execution would not have elevated the hated Jefferson to the presidency. In any case, the split in Federalist ranks contributed greatly to Jefferson's becoming President in the election of 1800.

The period between 1794 and 1800 was a period of growth in the organization of both political parties. Each party had recognized leaders and an identifiable press. Though there were no platforms as such, the programs of the parties were well advertised through newspapers, the distribution of pamphlets, and correspondence. By the end of the period well-established communications patterns were developed between central leaders and those on the state and local level, and Republicans and Federalists alike understood the principle of keeping a wavering congressman or senator in line by stirring up pressures from his home constituency. . . .

Jeffersonians entered the campaign of 1800 united and on the offensive, while the Federalists were handicapped by the now unbridgeable schism between Adams and the High Federalists. The Republican caucus again nominated Jefferson and Burr. The Hamiltonian faction at first attempted to replace Adams on the Federalist ticket: the aged Washington (who died before the election) was urged to run instead. He refused. Finally a caucus of Federalist members of Congress agreed to back Adams for President and Charles C. Pinckney for Vice President. Hamilton and his friends again tried the tactic of 1796, that is, to induce some

Federalist electors to vote for Pinckney and not for Adams. Before the campaign was over, Adams and Hamilton were publicly castigating each other in terms usually saved for the opposing party. Because of the very moderation of his policy, Adams retained the support of most Federalist leaders of the middle and lower rank.

The Republicans did not lack substantive issues. They made the most of an unsuccessful attempt by Federalists in Congress to create an electoral commission whose function would be to declare the Federalist candidates victorious, whatever the electoral count. The Sedition Act was now almost universally hated outside of New England, and its application in an election year made votes everywhere for the Republican cause. Federal expenses had doubled in the four preceding years as a consequence of military expenditures made to defend the country, or to wage war, against France. Adams' decision for peace gave the Republicans an excellent campaign issue. They argued that the new taxes, including the hated tax on land, houses, and slaves, had always been unnecessary. Jefferson vigorously publicized his insistence on "a government rigorously frugal and simple" and free of debt; a drastically reduced navy and dependence for internal defense on the state militias except in case of actual invasion; free commerce with all nations but political connections with none; and freedom of religion and the press, including repeal of the Sedition Act.

Despite Federalist disunity the election returns of 1800 were close. Jefferson and Burr won over Adams and Pinckney by a vote of 73 to 65. The sectional alignment was clear: Federalists swept New England, and Republicans won all but four of the southern electoral votes. Maryland split her votes evenly. A clean Republican victory in New York and a partial one in Pennsylvania insured the victory for Jefferson and Burr.

But one more crisis had to be faced. Since Jefferson and Burr had an equal number of electoral votes, the choice of who would be President, who Vice President, fell to the House of Representatives, each state having a single vote. And it was the lame-duck Federalist House, not the new heavily Republican one, that was to make the choice. Though it was clear that the country (and the electors) assumed that Jefferson would be President, High Federalists schemed to turn the highest office over to Burr. Others sought a deadlock until Jefferson would commit himself to the continuation of Federalist policies—the enlarged navy, for example. But Jefferson refused to make any commitment; and the issue remained in doubt for seventeen days and through thirty-five inconclusive roll calls in the House. Finally the majority of the voting states elected Jefferson, but only after Federalists from South Carolina, Vermont, and Maryland refrained from voting. At last and in high tension the first fundamental change of leaders took place in the new American nation.

ANTI-PARTY ATTITUDES IN AMERICA

7 FROM *Richard Hofstadter*
The Idea of a Party System

When Thomas Jefferson thought of setting down the lasting achievements he wanted inscribed on his tombstone, he mentioned the writing of the Declaration of Independence and of the Virginia Statute of Religious Liberty and the founding of the University of Virginia—thus omitting almost flamboyantly all the accomplishments of his long career in national politics. Yet surely this democrat and libertarian might have taken justifiable pride in his part in creating the first truly popular party in the history of the Western world, and in his leading role in the first popular election of modern times in which the reins of government were peacefully

SOURCE. Richard Hofstadter, *The Idea of a Party System: the Rise of Legitimate Opposition in the United States, 1780-1840,* pp. 1-3, 8-13, 16-18, 22-4, 27, 29, 34-5, 39 (Berkeley: University of California Press, 1969).

surrendered by a governing party to an opposition. Jefferson did
more than assert the claims of democracy: he was also a central
figure in developing responsible constitutional opposition, an
accomplishment which alone would grace any man's tombstone.

But here we are brought face to face with the primary paradox
of this inquiry: Jefferson, the founder, or more accurately, co-
founder, of the first modern popular party, had no use for political
parties. This seeming inconsistency is but one aspect of a larger
problem: the creators of the first American party system on both
sides, Federalists and Republicans, were men who looked upon
parties as sores on the body politic.

Political discussion in eighteenth-century England and America
was pervaded by a kind of anti-party cant. Jonathan Swift, in his
Thoughts on Various Subjects, had said that "Party is the madness of
many, for the gain of the few." This maxim, which was repeated
on this side of the Atlantic by men like John Adams and William
Paterson, plainly struck a deep resonance in the American mind.
Madison and Hamilton, when they discussed parties or factions
(for them the terms were usually interchangeable) in *The Federalist,*
did so only to arraign their bad effects. In the great debate over
the adoption of the Constitution both sides spoke ill of parties.
The popular sage, Franklin (who was not always consistent on the
subject), gave an eloquent warning against factions and "the
infinite mutual abuse of parties, tearing to pieces the best of
characters." George Washington devoted a large part of his
political testament, the Farewell Address, to stern warnings against
"the baneful effects of the Spirit of Party." His successor, John
Adams, believed that "a division of the republic into two great
parties. . .is to be dreaded as the greatest political evil under our
Constitution." Similar admonitions can be found in the writings of
the arch-Federalist Fisher Ames and the "philosopher of Jeffersonian democracy," John Taylor of Caroline. If there was one point
of political philosophy upon which these men, who differed on so
many things, agreed quite readily, it was their common conviction
about the baneful effects of the spirit of party.

That the anti-party thought and partisan action of the Founding Fathers were at odds with each other is not altogether
surprising. What they were trying to resolve—and they did so, after

all, with a substantial measure of success—is a fundamental problem of modern democracy.

The idea of a legitimate opposition—recognized opposition, organized and free enough in its activities to be able to displace an existing government by peaceful means—is an immensely sophisticated idea, and it was not an idea that the Fathers found fully developed and ready to hand when they began their enterprise in republican constitutionalism in 1788. We will misunderstand their politics badly if we read them so anachronistically as to imagine that they had a matured conception of a legitimate organized opposition or of a party system. Such a conception would certainly have engendered different political ideas and would probably have brought about different political practices. The Federalists and Republicans did not think of each other as alternating parties in a two-party system. Each side hoped instead to eliminate party conflict by persuading and absorbing the more acceptable and "innocent" members of the other; each side hoped to attach the stigma of foreign allegiance and disloyalty to the intractable leaders of the other, and to put them out of business as a party. The high point in Federalist efforts in this direction came with the Alien and Sedition Acts of 1798. The high point in Republican efforts came after the Treaty of Ghent in 1814. Where the Federalists had failed, the Republicans succeeded: the one-party period that came with the withering away of Federalism was seen by the Republicans not as an anomalous or temporary, much less as an undesirable eventuality, but as evidence of the correctness of their views and of the success of the American system.

If we inquire into the place of parties in Anglo-American thought during the eighteenth century, the root idea we find is that parties are evil. It is true, as Caroline Robbins has taken pains to show, that even before Edmund Burke's striking statement in behalf of the party principle in 1770, there was in England a somewhat stronger strain of dissent from this root idea than many historians have recognized. In the two centuries before 1770, she remarks, "some commentators and a larger number of participants in English political life had realized the existence of parties, had accepted with varying degrees of enthusiasm or fatalism the role of parties in a free state, and had developed theories about their function and to a lesser degree their control." But she emphasizes that these men "were many fewer than those who condemned party and faction, advocated uniformity of opinion and praised nonpartisan public service," and even when due credit is given to the strain of dissent that she records, we are left with the acknowledged fact that it was the dissent of a small minority. For the most part, as we shall see, men did not ask whether parties were good or bad. They asked only whether parties must be accepted as necessary evils in a free polity or whether it is in fact possible to prevent, abolish, or suppress them in the interests of a more pervasive harmony and unity in the state.

The very terms, "party" and "faction," which were used by some writers interchangeably, carried invidious overtones, though this is more regularly true of "faction." That word, in fact, seems to have had the meaning of a more sinister version of "party"— party functioning at its worst. Thus the standard anti-party writer, Bolingbroke, could say: "Faction is to party what the superlative is to the positive: party is a political evil, and faction is the worst of all parties." It was only in a much later period that faction came to mean simply and clearly what it now means to us—a subdivision of a larger party, or a party within a party. Nathan Bailey's *The New Etymological Dictionary*, published in its second edition in London in 1770, treated "party" and "faction" as synonyms. In Samuel Johnson's famous *Dictionary of the English Language* (London edition, 1822), faction is given two meanings: (1) a party in a state, and (2) tumult, discord, dissention. Most American writers seem to have assimilated these two senses of the word to each other. . . .

Before going on to the various refinements of the central proposition of the mischievous effects of party, it is important to be clear why the anti-party thinkers in the main stream of Anglo-American thought considered party an evil. It must be remembered here that American thought on this subject drew on English experience, and that most Englishmen looked back with relief upon the passing of that long, convulsive epoch of English history that occupied the seventeenth century and the first two decades of the eighteenth, in which they saw clear party divisions at work, with consequences they disliked to contemplate. "By 1688," as J. H. Plumb has observed, "violence in politics was an Englishman's birthright." "Conspiracy and rebellion, treason and plot, were a part of the history and experience of at least three generations of Englishmen." Impeachment or attainder, exile or death had at times been the penalties paid by the losers; and the opposition of the 1640's was, of course, associated with a most violent outcome. Party was associated with painfully deep and unbridgeable differences in national politics, with religious bigotry and clerical animus, with treason and the threat of foreign invasion, with instability and dangers to liberty. Even in 1715 the Tories, the opposition party, could still be seen as quasi-treasonable.

Finally, the party, with its capacity to arouse malice and hostility and to command loyalty to a political entity much narrower and less legitimate than the "public good" as a whole, was considered to be a force directly counterposed to civic virtue. Party loyalty was thought of as an insidious alternative to that disinterested good judgment on behalf of the public welfare that might be expected, in the absence of party forces, from the good citizen. This conception readily crossed the Atlantic. When the eighteenth-century American thought of a great and good man, he thought of a man free from such distortions of judgment. A contemporary, for example, praised the leading Virginia planter, Edmund Pendleton, in these terms: "None of his opinions were drawn from personal views or party prejudices. He never had a connexion with any political party,. . .so that his opinions were the result of his own judgment, and that judgment was rendered upon the best unbiased estimate he could make of the publick good." In 1807 Washington Irving could still say of a character in the *Salmagundi Papers*: "He pledged himself never to engage in party schemes, or party politics, but to stand up solely for the broad interests of his country."

As one reads eighteenth-century American writers with an eye to their borrowings from English thought, one finds that there were three archetypal views of party. I say archetypal with special emphasis: my main concern here is to set forth certain basic views, as abstractions. It is easier to classify the possible views of party in the framework of eighteenth-century thought than it is to classify most individual writers with confidence. On this subject many men were equivocal or inconsistent, and some on occasion changed their minds. . . .

First, there was the orthodox view, which in England was

identified especially with Bolingbroke [First Viscount, 1678-1751] and which in America, despite its general currency, may be called for convenience the Hamiltonian view—that parties are evils that can be avoided or abolished or suppressed, even if this must be done, paradoxically, through the temporary agency of a party of national unification. Suppose one begins with the widely shared proposition that parties are simply organizations formed to advance various special interests against the common public interest. One need then be disposed only slightly toward a belief in utopian solutions to hope that by some combination of devices parties can be got rid of. A minority—though surely not a negligible minority—of Anglo-American thinkers believed that this might actually be done. Whether cruder or gentler techniques were thought to be necessary to the end of getting rid of parties might depend upon the situation and temperament of the thinker, and on the kind of state apparatus he had in mind. Alexander Hamilton was among those who agreed that the elimination of parties was a possible goal in a well-designed and well-run state. "We are attempting by this Constitution," he said to the New York ratifying convention in 1788, "to abolish factions, and to unite all parties for the general welfare." In *The Federalist* he spoke of the value of a confederation in "suppressing" faction, or again of "repressing" it, and still again, in quoting Montesquieu, of "quelling" it. His rhetoric here is colored by a touch of force, as it is when he speaks of a strong American union as "a barrier against domestic faction and insurrection"—a significant coupling—or when, talking about the dangers of sedition, he promises that the Union will be an over-match for "a turbulent faction in any of the states."

It may occasion some surprise to revert to these anti-party statements from Hamilton, whom we think of as having become a fierce partisan and a party organizer. In fact, however, the whole tradition of anti-party writing is full of the works of men who were strong partisans; this tradition is, in very large part, the work of partisan writers and political leaders who are actually appealing to a general distrust of the idea of party in order to subvert some particular party or to advance the interest of another party whose greatest claim to glory is that it will surmount and eliminate the party battle itself.

In some ways the Jeffersonian who most resembles Bolingbroke is [James] Monroe. Bolingbroke, hedging in a manner characteristic of partisan anti-party thinkers, believed that a role of temporary usefulness could be served by a "country party" formed not on particular prejudices but "on principles of common interest." Such a party, he hastened to add, would not really be a party: "A party thus constituted, is improperly called party. It is the nation speaking and acting in the discourse and conduct of particular men." Monroe too was articulate about the role of the unifying party—and in the United States the Republicans were the "country party" as the Federalists were the "court party." It is party *conflict* that is evil, Monroe postulated, but a single party may be laudable and useful, even though not as a permanent instrument of the state, *if* it can make itself universal and strong enough to embody the common interest and to choke party strife.

Second among conceptions of party is the view—which in America could be called Madisonian, in England Humean—that though parties are indeed evil, their existence is an unavoidable by-product of a free state, and that they must therefore be endured with patience by all men who esteem liberty. The evils of party are thus held to be part of the price one pays for liberty. One can check and limit parties, but one cannot hope to do away with them.

This conception is usually accompanied by, indeed rooted in, a psychological assumption: the impulse to differ, and in differing to form parties, is founded in human nature. Or, as Madison put it in the Tenth *Federalist*, "the latent causes of faction are. . .sown in the nature of man." If so, nothing but the iron hand of tyranny can put faction down, and the evils of tyranny are far worse than those of faction.

David Hume was probably the only eighteenth-century English thinker of major consequence who hoped to control parties through a constitutional balance—the solution taken over and introduced into American thought most articulately by Madison. To the problems of politics Hume brought the attitude of the rationalist and the skeptic who was revolted by the bigoted party politics of the English past and by what he regarded as clerically inspired partisan fanaticism. In this respect, he was on common ground with Bolingbroke, but he also anticipated Edmund Burke's

sense that if parties were now to be liberated from the fundamentally divisive, emotionally searing issues that had plagued the
seventeenth century, they were far more susceptible to adequate
control than in the past.

Jefferson was among those who shared the Hume-Madison view,
though not at all times with consistency. One of the more
persistent notes in his writing is the common notion that parties
are founded in human nature, a notion very often supplemented in
his letters by the suggestion that it is a *twofold* party division that
is really nature—that men are, by instinct or impulse, natural
Whigs or Tories depending upon their disposition to trust and
"cherish" the people or to distrust and fear them. Hence it would
be of little point to talk of preventing parties altogether, though
Jefferson too had some hope that a well-designed constitution and
a healthy state of public opinion would check the worst evils of
party. . . .His basic conceptions of man and of political theory
pointed toward the Madison—Hume view of parties; but his
inability as a partisan to see any legitimacy in the Federalist party
brought about a quiet drift toward the Monrovian view.

Third among conceptions of party is the view—identified with
[Edmund] Burke in England, and in America, so far as I am
aware, with no one clearly and consistently among Jefferson's
contemporaries—that parties are not only inevitable but necessary
and, on balance, good. In his *Thoughts on the Cause of the Present
Discontents* (1770), Burke for the first time cut through the prevailing anti-party cant to make the case for party principles and
loyalties. . . .

In eighteenth-century America we cannot find a major thinker
to set down as Burke's counterpart, as we can set down Madison
for Hume or any one of several writers for Bolingbroke. Burke's
great statement on prt es came too late to be an influence in its
own right, for by 1770 the Americans of Jefferson's generation
were busy not with questions raised by party conflict but with the
forging of national unity and the pursuit of the rights of man.
Twenty years later, when they were ready to consider the problem
of party in a new light, Burke was on the verge of losing whatever
authority he might have had with men in the Jeffersonian ranks
because of his position on the French Revolution; and the
Federalists, who might otherwise have found him more congenial,

were, as the party in power, locked more firmly than ever into the notion that party was faction and that opposition was sedition.

A few observers, then, saw that parties could be good because instead of making for aggrandizement of power they offered another possible source of checks and balances in addition to those already built into the constitutional structure. A few others saw the value of opposition, short of party organization. So far as I have been able to determine, none saw that parties might perform a wide variety of positive functions necessary to representative democracy and unlikely to be performed as well by any other institutions. This seems more understandable when we consider not only the state of party in eightent-century thought but also the state of party development in eighteenth-century practice. The Founding Fathers did not have, in their current experience or historical knowledge, models of working parties that would have encouraged them to think in such terms. First, parties had to be created; and then at last they would begin to find a theoretical acceptance.

FEDERALISTS, REPUBLICANS: WHO WAS WHO?

8   FROM   *David Hackett Fischer*
            The Revolution of American Conservatism

The difficult problem of defining Federalism in social terms was not central to this project. Nevertheless, relevant material of two kinds came to light—impressionistic opinions of Federalists and Jeffersonians, and fragmentary election returns. The evidence is grossly incomplete, and conclusions from it are necessarily tentative. But on the theory that it is better to light one candle than to curse the darkness, they are offered here, for whatever they may be worth.

There were many patterns of political allegiance—all of them intricate in the extreme. Taken together, they present a picture of

SOURCE. David Hackett Fischer, *The Revolution of American Conservatism: the Federalist Party in the Era of Jeffersonian Democracy,* pp. 201, 203-6, 208-9, 211-17, 223-6 (New York: Harper and Row, 1965). Copyright c 1965 by David Hackett Fischer. Reprinted by permission of the publisher.

bewildering, disheartening complexity. Each serves to qualify all others; they lie superimposed one upon another, blending, shading, mixing, merging in an infinity of shapes and colors. But notwithstanding their complexity, clear patterns do appear, and some patterns are clearly more important than others. Contemporaries described them, and we can detect them in election returns. The object here is to discuss them in order of importance—to peel them back, one by one, with all due care for their fragility, caution for their intricacy and respect for many researchers who have gone before.

The most pervasive pattern of partisan allegiance derived from the existence of established and entrenched elites in the new republic. Americans who analyzed the structure of their society sometimes divided it into two groups—the better sort and the meaner sort, the respectable and the ambitious. "Society consists of two classes," a Friend of Order declared, "of those who have something and want to keep it, and of the rabble who have got nothing and are ever ready to be stirred up to get it."

The distinction, of course, was not between those who had something and those who had nothing, not simply between wealth and poverty, but between attainment and aspiration, between those who had and those who hungered. The most hungry, the most ambitious, the most "mean" from an elitist perspective were men who had much and wanted more—men who wished to add respectability to riches, or riches to popular influence. Thus conceived, the political pattern was clear. The established elites in most states were Federalist; their challengers were Jeffersonian. Recent students of the period, even those most critical of [Charles A.] Beard's generalizations, would appear to accept this one. . . .

It goes without saying that Federalists claimed the elites as their own. "Here as everywhere," a Connecticut gentleman wrote, "the men of talents, information and property, yea and I may add honesty and integrity are found among the Federalists." Their claims were recognized by Jeffersonians, who used different value-terms but to describe the same facts. A New England Republican labeled the Federalists of his town the "prigarchy." John Binns of Pennsylvania conceded that Federalism commanded the support of "everything that considers itself a part of the natural aristocracy." A Jeffersonian editor in Delaware wrote, "The Federalists boasted that the weight of talents is on their side; it cannot be denied that this has been the case." In South Carolina, Charles Pinckney, "Blackguard Charlie," the family Democrat, acknowledged "the weight of talent, wealth, and personal and family influence brought against us".

Federalists could not, of course, claim that all of the wealth of the nation was behind them. "Rich, overgrown rich men are to be found among every description of politics," a New York Federalist declared. But Friends of Order could claim most of the old wealth of the republic, and once again their claims were ratified by opponents. William Bentley, a Republican, noted that his party had "rich men not high in reputation." Many a Federal family sought to stave off the challenge of new-rich Republican rivals. The Derbys and Crowninshields of Salem are surely the most conspicuous examples. The gentry of Baltimore county, the Howards and Ridgelys and Carrolls, unwillingly surrendered their local power to parvenu Republican merchants such as the Smiths and McKims. In New Castle County, Delaware, new manufacturing families such as the Du Ponts were Republican; their influence rapidly outran that of the older Federalist gentry. The Browns of Providence faced, and outfaced, a host of rising Republican merchants and manufacturers. Jeffersonian *arrivistes* in Pittsburgh were not welcomed to the drawing rooms and dancing assemblies of the Federalist "connexion" nor into the commercial affairs of the town; and at the opposite end of Pennsylvania, Stephen Girard suffered similar snubs from Philadelphia Federalists. . . .

A sense of elitism derived not merely from old wealth but from occupation as well. Men who held positions of power and prominence in 1800 tended toward Federalism. The same qualifications entered above also apply here, of course. Inherited power operated like ancient riches, to distinguish old families from new. Republicans, Federalists, and neutral observers agreed. John Binns of Pennsylvania, who declared that "everything that considers itself a part of the natural aristocracy" tended toward Federalism, defined aristocracy in occupational terms—"nearly all the lawyers, nearly all the merchants, most of the parsons, many of the physicians". . . .

Patterns among artisans, craftsmen, and petty shopkeepers reflect the same general theme. Occupations which appeared least "respectable," and most mobile though not necessarily the most impoverished, were markedly enthusiastic for Jefferson. The butchers of Philadelphia, often affluent but rarely respectable, were "distinguished among their fellow-citizens, for their support and attachment to Republican principles." The cartmen of New York City showed similar political attitudes. "Indigo pedlars" in Connecticut, who were regarded as a species of gypsy by the sober citizenry of that stable and conservative state, were decidedly Democratic in 1800.

The colleges of the new nation were, if not Federalist, at least decidedly hostile to Jefferson. The trend was most apparent in New England institutions but by no means confined to them alone. A Princeton undergraduate wrote in 1800 that "the students are in general on the federal side; this cannot, I fear, be said of the people at large." Similar evidence exists for Columbia, Brown, and even the new colleges in North Carolina, Georgia, and later in Kentucky. An exception was William and Mary, where the students refused to wear crepe for the death of Washington and received the news of Jefferson's election with "joy almost bordered on madness."

The class of men denominated "gentlemen" could not, of course account for all of the votes which Federalist candidates received in 1800. A geographical analysis of voting patterns in the elections of that year suggest that particularly heavy concentrations of Federalist voters were to be found in the following areas:

1. The North Shore of New England, including Essex County, Mass., Rockingham and Hillsborough Counties, N.H., and York and Cumberland Counties, Maine.

2. The Connecticut River Valley, including Hartford County, Conn., Worcester and Hampshire Counties in Massachusetts, Grafton and Cheshire Counties in New Hampshire and Windham, Windsor, and Caledonia Counties in Vermont.

3. The middle counties of Rhode Island—Kent and Bristol.

4. The old Dutch counties of the Hudson Valley, including Columbia, Rensselaer, and Albany Counties in New York and Bergen County in New Jersey.

5. The counties of West Jersey, and the central portions of that state—Burlington, Somerset, Middlesex, Monmouth, Hunterdon, Gloucester, Salem, Cumberland, and Cape May.

6. Philadelphia and the southeastern counties of Pennsylvania, including Adams, Chester, Delaware, and Lancaster.

7. Luzerne County in northeastern Pennsylvania.

8. The "Delmarva" Peninsula, as it is now called, including Kent and Sussex Counties in Delaware; Dorchester, Worcester, and Somerset Counties in Maryland, and Virginia's Accomack and Northampton Counties.

9. Tidewater Maryland and Virginia—Charles, St. Mary's, and Prince George's Counties in the former state, Loudoun, Westmoreland, Fairfax, Stafford, James City, New Kent, Henrico, and Charles City Counties in the Old Dominion.

10. The upper Cape Fear counties of North Carolina, in Fayetterille and Salisbury Districts.

11. The southern coastal counties of North Carolina, in New Bern and Wilmington Districts.

12. The South Carolina low country, including Cheraw and Georgetown, Charleston, and Orangeburg and Beaufort Districts.

13. The Valley of Virginia, western Virginia, and western Maryland, including Alleghany County Md., and Hampshire, Hardy, Pendleton, Augusta, Rockbridge, and Greenbrier Counties in Virginia.

There are other patterns which appear more clearly in the voting returns for 1800. Most of the Federalist regions enumerated above had one set of characteristics in common, they were mature, static, homogeneous, and ingrown. Jeffersonian areas on the other hand tended to be immature, fluid, and dynamic.

The most staunchly Federalist region in the nation was the Connecticut River Valley. Timothy Dwight wrote of it, "The inhabitants of the valley might be said in several respects to possess a common character; and, in all the different states resemble each other more than their fellow citizens, who live on the coast. This similarity is derived from their descent, their education, their local circumstances, and their mutual intercourse. In the older settlements most of the inhabitants are natives of this valley, and those who are not, yield to the influence of a character which they continually see all around them."

Jeffersonian areas, on the other hand, appear to have shown a different set of characteristics. Timothy Dwight's notorious comments upon that "Nazareth of anti-Federalism," western Vermont, as populated by "the discontented, the enterprising, the ambitious and the covetous," may perhaps be taken as something more than a measure of one Federalist's irascibility. Dynamism, expansion, and mobility appear, generally, to have distinguished Republican regions from those in which Federalism flourished.

Impressionistic evidence is reinforced by demographic statistics. The single variable which correlates more closely than any other with voting behavior in 1800 is the rate of population growth as revealed in the censuses of 1790, 1800, and 1810. The most Federalist state in the nation, Connecticut, had the smallest growth rate—6 per cent in the 1790s, 4 per cent in the first decade of the nineteenth century. Population increase in the Connecticut Valley (except its northernmost reaches) was equally small in the period 1800-1810: 6 per cent in Worcester County, Massachusetts; 5 per cent in Hampshire County, Massachusetts; 2 per cent in Cheshire County, New Hampsire; 4 per cent in Windham County, Vermont; and 7 percent in Windsor County, Vermont.

In the middle states, the same generalizations can be made. The most Federal counties of New York were Albany and Columbia; the first was nearly static (2 per cent population rise, 1800-1810) and in the second, population was actually declining. Rensselaer and Washington Counties, also Federalist, showed higher rates of population increase (20 and 23 per cent respectively in 1800-1810) but were still far behind the extraordinary New York average, 78 per cent. In New Jersey the three decidedly Republican counties of Morris, Essex and Sussex had growth rates of 23, 17 and 13 per cent; the Federalist counties of Bergen, Burlington, and Hunterdon had rates of 10, 13 and 14 per cent. Federalist counties in southeastern Pennsylvania—Adams, Delaware, Chester, and Lancaster—showed increases of 10-23 per cent between 1800 and 1810, in a state which was growing at the rate of 35 per cent.

States south of the Mason-Dixon line were much the same. In Delaware's one Republican county, Newcastle, growth rate during the 1790s was 30 per cent; in Federalist Kent County population increase in the same period was 3 per cent, and in Sussex the population was declining. Maryland's Republican counties were growing rapidly; Federalist counties in southern Maryland were losing population. Alleghany County in western Maryland, decidedly Federalist, was not a frontier area, as has sometimes been suggested, but a stagnant backwater in which population was also falling. Federalist Virginia—the Eastern shore, Potomac Valley, and the tidewater counties—was in process of depopulation. In western Virginia, the counties which showed heavy concentrations of Federalists—Berkeley, Hampshire, Hardy, Pendleton, Bath, Augusta, Rockbridge, Botetourt, and Greenbrier—were altogether losing population during the decade 1800-1810. In North Carolina, Republican Districts such as Hillsborough and Morgan were increasing during the 1790s at the rates of 34 and 47 per cent; Federalist areas—New Bern, Wilmington, and Fayetteville—were increasing at rates of 9, 15, and 21 per cent.

There were exceptions, of course. Grafton, Rockingham, and Hillsborough Counties in New Hampshire, Cumberland County in Maine, Caledonia and Orleans in Vermont, Oneida, Ontario, Steuben, Chenango, and Tioga Counties in New York, Luzerne County in Pennsylvania, and the Salisbury District in North Carolina were areas with high rates of population increase which voted Federalist in 1800. Nearly all of them, however would shift to the Republican side within two or three years.

Population increase would appear to be a more significant indicator than length of settlement or density of population. The southeastern counties of Massachusetts, for example, appear to have been surprisingly dynamic. And it might seem at first sight that that the lower Hudson counties of New York, with Long Island, should have been as mature, stable, and static as the middle Hudson counties which voted Federalist. But these southern counties, particularly Suffolk, Queens, Kings, and Westchester, had been the scene of extensive confiscations of loyalist property which by the 1790s were beginning to be broken up into smaller holdings. Census returns for all these counties show growth rates of 10 to 50 per cent. Similarly, the most dynamic urban areas tended to be Jeffersonian—Baltimore, a rough, disorderly boom-town in the new republic, was decidedly Republican. Philadelphia, increasing more slowly, was Federalist.

Ethnic voting patterns in 1800 were clear to contemporary observers of political behavior. The Irish, who were beginning to pour into the great "flour cities" of the middle states and into New England as well, were overwhelmingly Republican. Many were political refugees; all felt the bite of prejudice in the Anglo-American republic. There were the inevitable exceptions—Irishmen such as Thomas Fitzsimons who had emigrated before the War of Independence and became an important Federalist in Pennsylvania. But Republicans and Federalists agreed upon the rule.

French immigrants appear to have been as generally Republican as the Irish, notwithstanding an occasional *emigre* who became a "friend of order and good government." Of 311 Frenchmen who voted in Charleston in 1812, all but seven favored the Republican ticket. The six or seven hundred Frenchmen who had settled in Philadelphia by 1808 were reported to be nearly unanimous for the Democratic cause.

The Germans of Pennsylvania and Maryland had generally voted for Federalist candidates in the mid 1790s, but in 1800 were generally, if not enthusiastically, Republican. Contemporaries explained the shift as a reaction to the threat of direct taxation and to the repression of Fries' Rebellion. In 1805 they would show a clear perference for moderate rather than radical Republicans. In 1814, the threat of Republican taxes [during the War of 1812] would drive many of them back to the Federalists.

Free Negroes, in the states which permitted them to vote, appear to have been divided; torn, perhaps, between the ideals of the Republican movement and its slave-owning leadership. Courted by both parties on election day, spurned by both parties through the rest of the year, they appear to have split their votes.

Only two non-English ethnic groups leaned to Federalism in 1800 and afterwards: the old Dutch families of the Hudson valley, and Scottish merchants and factors who were sufficiently numerous to be politically significant in Richmond, Norfolk, New Bern, Wilmington, Charleston, and Savannah. Altogether, the party which in 1800 sometimes called itself "Federal-American" or "True-American" or "American-Republican" was deeply suspicious of all men who were not old-stock Anglo-American and received their hostility in turn.

Religious patterns were of great importance in 1800. In New England, the established Congregational churches were, despite recent attempts at reinterpretation, bastions of Federalism. But New England's establishments had acquired many enemies by

1800, both within and without their folds, and most were Jeffersonian. The ripples of revivalism which continued to overspread New England contributed to the fragmentation of the Congregational churches which had begun early in the century. And wherever a religious controversy appeared in the quiet New England countryside, it blurred into the partisan conflict. Specific alignments were difficult to predict, but from theological commitments one generalization is indisputable—a religious faction in Massachusetts, Connecticut, or New Hampshire which felt that it had more to gain than lose from a union of church and state was certain to be Federalist. Edwardsian Calvinists who suspected the establishments of a tendency toward Arminianism, Unitarianism, or worse were, in the judgement of Parson Bentley, more often Jeffersonian than not. On the other side, some Unitarians and many Universalists who found the prevailing temper of the established churches to be too orthodox, were, in John Adam's considered opinion, rarely in the Federal camp. And of course nearly all the sects and denominations which were expanding in New England were apt to be Jeffersonian—be they Irish Catholic or Anabaptist, Methodist or Episcopalian.

In other parts of the Union, three religious groups were generally Jeffersonian—Baptists, Jews, and Irish Catholics. The Baptist Church in Londonderry, Vermont, which excommunicated four of its members for joining the Washington Benevolent Society, appears to have been representative in its politics if not in its zeal. Even in Virginia it was said that Baptists were "almost universally Republican."

Two other religious groups were generally Federalist—Methodists on the Delmarva peninsula, and Scotch-Irish Presbyterians in western Virginia and the Cape Fear region of North Carolina. Jefferson himself wrote that "the string of counties at the Western foot of the Blue ridge settled originally by Irish presbyterians [composes] precisely the tory [Federalist] district of the state." Local historians have discussed the relevance of Methodism to Federalist strength in Delmarva, and of Presbyterianism in the Cape Fear region.

Each of these patterns, as has already been noted, served to qualify all the others. Men were caught up by them in different and often conflicting and sometimes unique ways. It remains only to remind the reader that these patterns are descriptive and not necessarily causal. Did men take possession of the land, or did the land take possession of them? Were they masters or servants of their interests? Dilemmas such as this cannot be resolved by appeals to historical evidence. The historian must yield to the theologian.

PART THREE
Uneven Development:
Parties in the States

Although it had its origins in the cockpit of national controversy, the first party system was also shaped by events and conditions in the several states. There were many variations, and party formation was markedly uneven from state to state.

A mixture of state and national concerns appears to have provided the stimuli for close party competition in New York. In effect the state faction of George Clinton, along with new elements including workingmen and the Tammany society under Aaron Burr, metamorphosed into the state's Republican party. The old Schuylerite and Hamiltonian factions, meanwhile, provided the core of an effective Federalist force. Yet long-standing divisions between New Yorkers were supplemented by new conflicts over issues of world politics. Such issues, according to Alfred F. Young, gave the Republicans a "mass following." Even so, it was not until the Federalists failed to deliver the state's electoral vote in 1800 that New York became a basically Republican state. If the New York Republicans "cannot accurately be called the New York Jeffersonians," they provided Jefferson and his party with a crucial increment of strength.

The transition from faction to party in Massachusetts also proceded on a dual basis. In a fundamentally Federalist state by interest and sentiment, Republican growth in part depended on, and in part contributed to a gradual erosion of political deference in the Commonwealth. Nascent Republicans appealed particularly to citizens who were "alienated from established authority," as Paul Goodman puts it, and were "convinced that those long entrenched in positions of influence blocked the advancement of worthy and ambitious though less favored citizens." It was, in large part, an issue of open opportunity against traditional economic and social elites—or again, of "Establishment" and "anti-Establishment." By the mid-1790s, however, national issues and particularly the Jay Treaty controversy helped to advance party competition and party development. Men tended to respond to foreign and domestic issues in accord with their place in local society, and the hopes and fears that went with their social position. Republicans labored accordingly to break down "the barriers of advancement" at home, as they saw the French Revolution doing abroad. Yet their progress was slow. Only once, in 1804, did Massachusetts support a Republican presidential contender, although the Republicans won some state offices. They also elected some Congressmen, one of whom, Barnabas Bidwell, served as Jeffersonian leader in the House of Representatives.

To the South, the broad reaches of Virginia sustained the Republican faith. Although Federalists there could look to leaders like Patrick Henry and John Marshall, and had the support of many of the state's oldest families, they were never able seriously to threaten Jeffersonian hegemony. In comparison with New York and Massachusetts, there was also a more important difference. The home of Jefferson, Madison, John Taylor, Monroe, and John Randolph was not only the great source of national Republican leadership. Party formation in the Old Dominion was also overwhelmingly the product of national concerns, as Harry Ammon points out: indeed, the chief function of Virginia Republican endeavors was to provide not only leadership but "correct principles" for the national party. It was Hamilton's economic policy, with its implications of consolidated power, together with world politics and especially the Jay Treaty and its intimations of truckling to monarchy, that brought Virginia old republicans to new, Republican-party endeavors. These national questions were transposed to the state arena, where they became the major impetus for party formation. In the area of structure and organization, however, parties in Virginia were still comparatively backward. Virginia's economy and society remained relatively homogeneous; the easy tradition of deference to social elites continued even as carefully-devised "mass" meetings spread; and relatively low levels of competition and voting participation persisted in most elections. In short, there was little need for the more finely tuned party machinery that characterized more diverse communities.

In nearby Delaware, the smallest of the states in population, parties also formed around national and international issues. Delaware was so given to deference to high-toned family connections that Jefferson referred to it as virtually "a county of England." It was also heavily Federalist; and yet there was more than "one d—n democrat" in the state, to use an irate Federalist's language. Republican strength was concentrated in the northernmost of Delaware's three counties, New Castle. More diverse in its economy, ethnic and religious mixture, and social structure than the rest of the state, it was, moreover, less deferential than the more-southern, agricultural counties. It was also marked by the city of Wilmington, where the pro-Jeffersonian DuPont dynasty built their first powder mill in 1802. By joining their strength in New Castle with voters elsewhere who had begun to chafe at old-family domination, the Republicans were able to score a few victories now and then. Their chief leader, Caesar A. Rodney, won a place in the national House of Representatives and became Republican floor leader. Even so, Delaware never once voted for a Jeffersonian candidate for president. In its basic partisan stance, it remained the Federalist redoubt of the middle states.

Differences from state to state have always characterized the substructures of America's political parties. The variations that the first party system exhibited provided a useful and fascinating laboratory for comparative political analysis.

PARTY RIVALRY IN
NEW YORK

9 FROM *Alfred F. Young*
The Democratic Republicans of New York

What were the issues which gave rise to the Democratic-
Republican movement. . .? Noble Cunningham's generalizations
that the Republican party was "a product of national rather than
state politics" and that it "was a new growth that sprang from the
divisions in Congress and the national government" must be
modified for New York, perhaps even more than he concedes. In
New York. . .the Republican party was built around the core of
the anti-Federalist Clintonian party, the product of Governor
Clinton's long tenure in the state government. Men who were
attracted to Clinton by his policies and patronage, his principles

SOURCE. Alfred F. Young, *The Democratic Republicans of New York: the Origins 1763-
1797,* pp. 570-78 (Chapel Hill: University of North Carolina Press, 1967). Reprinted
by permission of the University of North Carolina Press, the author, and the
Institute of Early American History and Culture.

93

and reputation, did not need national issues to stimulate them to
oppose the Federalists, their traditional political enemies. . . .

The national policies which did affect New York during Washington's first administration operated differently than most historians have assumed. The "high tone" of the new government, the "aristocracy" that loomed so large in Senator Maclay's diary simply did not strike fire as a public issue. Neither did Hamiltonian finance, at least not at its inception. . . .

The issue of banking, combined with assumption, was. . .important for providing the occasion on which the Livingstons first demonstrated their opposition to Hamilton's policies. There is a more complex explanation for Chancellor [Robert R.] Livingston's departure from the house of Federalism than his disappointment over not being appointed to high office. An ally of Governor Clinton in the Revolution, he had been slow to join Hamilton and Jay in the battle for a new federal Constitution. He had fought Hamilton on banking policy in 1784; he never favored assumption of the state debts; he also had a latent disagreement with John Jay over the French alliance. Principle thus combined with pique and pride. After 1793 when foreign affairs became crucial, Washington found that he could not bridge the gap between the Chancellor and the Federalists by patronage.

The "republican interest" that came into existence in Washington's first term would not have found a mass following had it not been for Federalist foreign policies in the second. Here the stimulus was unmistakably national and international. The French Revolution helped but it was not as divisive an issue in New York as dramatizers of the period have made it out to be. It operated, moreover, to widen a long-standing schism over the French alliance in which Robert R. Livingston, the "gallican," and John Jay, the "anti-Gallican," had long been protagonists. British policy on the high seas and on the frontier, coupled with the Federalist response to them, created the Republican movement in New York, enabling Republicans to catch full sail the strongest winds of nationalism to blow across American political waters since the Revolution.

After a political following was handed to them by the Federalists, the New York Republicans, it must be said, bungled their chance. They clung to Citizen Genet after Jefferson advised them to abandon him as a liability; Cornelia Clinton's marriage to the Frenchman was symbolic. They became strident "war hawks" in the spring of 1794, alienating both the commercial interest and the frontier, and by making a last-ditch fight against Jay's Treaty in 1796 they pitted themselves against George Washington whose prestige outmatched theirs. In each crisis Federalists were able to outmaneuver the Republicans, making the issue Washington or his traducers, and war or peace with Britain. The result in New York, as elsewhere, was that Republicans were unable to consolidate their gains of 1794, the year of patriotism, thus losing the crucial presidential and congressional elections of 1796.

This extraordinary support for the Federalist party, one of the striking themes of New York politics in the 1790's, was based in large part on the widespread conviction that Federalist policies benefited the state. Hamiltonian financial measures, while they feathered the nests of a good number of wealthy New Yorkers, were also to the advantage of the state treasury as a holder of federal securities and then as an investor in bank stock. The invigoration of commerce lined the pockets of exporting farmers as well as merchants. National military power broke the back of Indian resistance; and national diplomacy, however humiliating Jay's Treaty may otherwise have been, restored the forts on New York soil and established a procedure to indemnify shippers for their losses. The results were a boon to pioneer as well as proprietor on the frontier and to all in the east whose prosperity rested on foreign commerce. Federalists, in short, had an outstanding record to point to.

Secondly, Federalists, as the "outs" in the state government, exploited to the hilt Clinton's aberrations from democratic ideals. They campaigned against him for his excessive stay in office and his personal fortune. They hung the albatross of the land office sales of 1791 around his neck for a decade. They championed the "rights of suffrage" after the election "steal" of 1792.

Third, and most important, one face of Federalism was consistently moderate. Under the guidance of Hamilton, Schuyler, Jay, King, and Benson, the New York Federalists established a middle-of-the-road record on issue after issue. They promised amendments to the Constitution in 1788, toned down the "high" Federalists, and ran Robert Yates, a moderate anti-Federalist, against Clinton in 1789; they cooled off the western hotheads who wanted to oust Clinton by extra-legal methods after the election decision of 1792, and did an about-face in 1794, fortifying the state and adopting an embargo in order to avert war. This flexibility continued the tactic cultivated by conservative Whigs from the 1770's, based on the dictum of Robert R. Livingston to "yield to the torrent if they hoped to direct its course." John Jay's career is the perfect example of this policy.

On the other hand these same Federalists had a strain of contempt for the people—a class prejudice—which was a major cause of their undoing. "Aristocracy" was a persistent issue in a state which from 1777 on elected George Clinton because it did not want a Livingston or a Schuyler as governor. It took on new meaning in the 1790's in reaction to the highhandedness of Hudson Valley landlords, western land proprietors, and New York City magistrates. In 1795, Stephen Van Rensselaer, who coerced his tenants at the polls, barely sneaked in as lieutenant-governor. . . .

The violent reaction of Federalist leaders to the democratic upsurge of the mid-1790's revealed a growing rigidity. In stigmatizing the Democratic societies as "self created," the "town meetings" as the work of "the rabble," and petitions to Congress as unwarranted, Federalists asserted their elitist notion of representation. Lacking confidence in their ability to win back Republicans as they had once won over followers of the popular Whigs and anti-Federalists, New York's Federalists were on the path to repression which culminated in the Alien and Sedition Laws of 1798. Years later Noah Webster in counseling Rufus King on a way out of the political debacle to which such policies had led them, resorted to the very language Robert R. Livingston had used in 1777: "They have attempted to resist the force of current opinion instead of falling into the current with a view to direct it". . . . By then, however, it was too late.

By 1797 there clearly was a Democratic-Republican movement in New York State which embraced not only the Republican party but the Republican societies and the Republican press as well. The societies were distinct from the party, although they took part in elections on a *sub rosa* basis. But there were societies with staying power in only three counties who could not have had more than 500 members, all told. They were more "advanced" than the party and bore the stigma of "Jacobinism" which could not be pinned on local leaders elsewhere. They functioned as the "sentinels" who watched the rulers, as catalysts who produced the "addresses" to rally the citizenry, and as behind-the-scenes organizers. In New York City the Democratic society may be credited with perfecting the techniques of direct democratic expression: the "town meetings," the patriotic parades and celebrations, the circulation of public petitions.

By the end of the era of Washington, Republicans had more of the attributes of a political party than the anti-Federalists. They had a name—usually "Republican"; their candidates often ran on a clearly labeled ticket; committees whose personnel was fairly stable from year to year made their nominations and conducted their campaigns. If Republicans ran as individuals as most still 'did, it was because it was expedient to avoid the party label. But political leaders knew who "their" men were. There was a process in operation; it went further in some areas, New York City, for example, than others. It also went further in national than state elections. Gubernatorial elections were the least partisan, as is indicated by the efforts of Burr and Chancellor Livingston in 1795 to secure nominations from both "interests" and by the management of the campaign by "the friends of Mr. Yates" and the "friends of Mr. Jay." Yet while the lines were looser in state elections they were essentially the same as in national affairs. In 1796 assemblymen and state senators elected without a label lined up in the state legislature on a predictable partisan basis to choose presidential electors.

Republican campaign methods did not change markedly in this period. Campaign workers made more use of newspapers, pamphlets, and broadsides but they still knew the value of "a beaver hat, an oyster supper, or a glass of grog" to sway a voter. And while the voters heard more and more appeals to lofty principles, one suspects that in more than one township "a large majority gloried" at the election of their favorite because the legislature had located the new county courthouse favorably. On the other hand if campaign methods did not change, it was unquestionably true that more and more people participated in the political process: in making nominations, in campaigning, and in voting.

By virtue of their strength in the state the New York Republicans clearly were a component of a national party; indeed, the national party appears to have been no more than a loose amalgam of the state groups. Neither Jefferson nor Madison had anything to do with organizing the New York Republicans; there would have been a Republican party in New York without them. Nor did the New Yorkers follow Madison's lead either in the fight against Hamiltonian finance in 1789-90 or in the foreign policy crisis of 1794-96 when they took a position to the "left" of the Virginians. They willingly backed Jefferson for the presidency in 1796 because of his opposition to Federalism, not because of his influence among the state party leaders. The New York Democratic Republicans thus cannot accurately be called New York Jeffersonians.

MASSACHUSETTS:
ESTABLISHMENT VERSUS
ANTI-ESTABLISHMENT

10 FROM   *Paul Goodman*
          The Democratic-Republicans of Massachusetts

Toward the middle of the [1790's]. . .the nature of politics in
[Massachusetts] dramatically altered. Continuous parties emerged
based on competing interests and ideologies. Their origins cannot
be traced simply to an earlier factionalism or to an earlier conflict
of interests, for parties were new institutions which stemmed less
from old rivalries and issues than from fresh problems confronting
the nation. As long as interest groups remained content, politics
remained highly local, factious, and dull. But by the end of the
century, cataclysmic events abroad disrupted the entire Atlantic
world, threatened the nation's placid prosperity, polarized groups,
and plunged the young Republic into a decade of party warfare. . . .

Political parties were new groupings that differed from the
factions and interests of the past, though they often incorporated
such elements. Parties were more permanent and more heterogeneous, had broader objectives and far more elaborate organization, than earlier formations. Unlike factions, which were temporary alliances constantly in motion, seeking limited, often personal
advantages, parties held together large groups with common
objectives which sought political power to influence public policy.

SOURCE. Paul Goodman, *The Democratic-Republicans of Massachusetts: Politics in a
Young Republic,* pp. 51-2, 62-3, 70-1, 75-8, 85-6, 90-1, 94-6 (Cambridge: Harvard
University Press), copyright 1964, by the President and Fellows of Harvard College.

In contrast, factions had been loose aggregations of ambitious and skillful manipulators who thrived where the electorate was small or apathetic, where social groups were contented or at least disorganized and leaderless, and where the deference of the many for the few left the business of government to the management of an elite. Thus Governor Hancock had led a faction which successfully obtained office even though it represented no particular group in Massachusetts and favored no particular program other than the enjoyment of the privileges and honors of office. . . .

A party united a broad spectrum of interests, but it was more than simply a collection of these elements. In the past, interests had entered politics to influence government on behalf of a particular sector of society whose aims were specific and limited and whose political involvement was temporary. Parties, however, formed coalitions of diverse groups seeking to shape public policy through continuous political activity. Parties included factions and interests, but were more than the sum of their parts and had an institutional life of their own, including an organizational apparatus which nominated candidates, planned strategy and tactics, raised funds, and influenced public opinion. And partisans shared a zommon ideology which knit together far-flung interests, generated an emotional attachment to a cause (including its leaders and organization), and sustained continuous, intensive, and patterned modes of political rivalry.

The Democratic-Republican formation was a heterogeneous coalition of interests which cut across regional, economic, occupational, and religious lines. The party attracted persons alienated from established authority, convinced that those long entrenched in positions of influence blocked the advancement of worthy and ambitious though less favored citizens.

The party builders were not primarily national statesmen directing affairs from Philadelphia or professional politicians operating from Boston. Unlike later professional party leaders, they were generally ambitious merchants, tradesmen, capitalists, speculators, ministers, and office seekers who formed an interest and mobilized relatives, friends, acquaintances, and dependents to oppose those in power. As they fought for influence, they tried to swell the party showing at the polls by mustering wide support in the community. By linking together a varied collection of leaders and championing a broad spectrum of dissatisfied elements, the Republican party in Massachusetts formed a powerful alliance whose importance steadily mounted after 1800.

The common bond that united Republican Berkshire farmers with Salem merchants and rural Calvinists with urban rationalists was an interpretation of postrevolutionary experience. More than any other event, the French Revolution defined the content and style of politics. More than any other act, the Jay Treaty influenced the development of party. A strange and unreal debate developed in the 1790's which pictured two hostile groups, each dedicated to undermining the established order. Both linked their vision of the future and their understanding of the present with events abroad. . . .

Men's positions in the social structure shaped their responses to the events of the decade. Those most securely established in local office, trade, and finance, those controlling the seats of authority in church and state, came to view the French Revolution with horror. Fearing that involvement would undermine prosperity, they also believed that the spread of French doctrine threatened the social order. They recoiled from Jacobinism, clung to the protection of a British alliance, and attempted to uproot subversion at home. Well-placed individuals such as the judges, justices, probate officers, county treasurers, sheriffs, the complex array of entrenched officials together with the older county families and their professional and mercantile allies, led the Federalist party.

The sources of Republican leadership were different. The party attracted persons either outside the elite or enjoying a recently acquired and insecure position in local society. They were often new men who came from rising families that had been excluded from the highest levels of influence and standing. Frequently men of substance in their own communities, they desired but lacked county-wide influence, and unlike some of the newly arrived had not gained a firm position in the social order. Rising from obscurity or modest circumstances, they identified revolution and republicanism at home and abroad with opportunity. The French had uprooted privilege, destroyed ecclesiastical and monarchic establishments, and had given power to those who had been excluded for centuries. Americans who condemned change and feared and distrusted popular rule cast doubt on the validity of republicanism.

Federalism, according to Republicans, threatened the future of the newcomer, the ambitious man, the outsider. To a few, the Hamiltonian financial system spelled the creation of a monied aristocracy that would rule the land and widen the distinctions between various levels of society. Federalist partiality for Britain appeared to mark that corrupt kingdom as a model for American imitation. Federalist foreign policy moved the nation closer to war with France, bringing with it heavy taxes and the persecution of dissent. Federalist commercial policy doomed newly developed and profitable ties with France and the Continent. Within Massachusetts itself, Federalists hoarded power and privilege, narrowing rather than widening opportunity. The party stood for monopoly of local office, charter privileges, the natural resources of Maine, and the religious, institutional, and professional life of the community.

The nation was misruled, Republicans announced, because government did not truly reflect the interests of the people. Voters were often deceived and lacked direct representation. For generations they had submitted to a system of indirect rule whereby the lawyer, not the merchant, the local judge, not the farmer, sat in the General Court. But indirect government did not always work. It suffered anarchic breakdown in the 1780's and now a decade later once again was under heavy attack. Republicans repeatedly demanded direct representation. Communities should select men whose interests closely reflected those of the voters. Merchants, not lawyers, should sit for the trading towns; farmers, not judges, should represent the inland communities. Only then would an identity exist between voters and officials.

The Republican appeal was essentially an attack on traditional sources of leadership, not a call for social upheaval but a demand for enlarged opportunities for the excluded. Finding difficulty in meeting the argument, Federalists rehearsed the notion of a harmony of interest and denounced their critics as "ignorant rich men" eager for power. The Republican polemic proved to be more than shrewd propaganda: it worked. Merchants such as Orchard Cook and Jacob Crowninshield, farmers such as Joseph B. Varnum, and mechanics such as Thompson Skinner replaced many of the Federalist attorneys who sat in Congress. By questioning the assumption by which Federalists ruled, Republicans hoped to gain influence. The obstacles to opportunity must be weakened and above all the nation must avoid war with France and entanglement with Britain. The channels of trade with the Continent and the Far East must remain open; expansive measures must replace repressive political and economic ones; access to corporate privilege must become available to everyone; and the professional and communal life of the state must comprehend groups that had been excluded previously. These were the general objectives of the Republican interest; their precise formulation varied. Eastern merchants were concerned with foreign trade and sharing in grants of corporate charters, while their inland allies were moved by other problems. But everywhere Jeffersonians joined to remove the barriers to advancement.

After two decades of struggle, the party enjoyed considerable success. In many communities Republicans became the dominant group, replacing the older leadership or at least sharing influence. In time they merged into the social order and eventually distinctions blurred and became almost imperceptible. Party labels lost their meaning as the older differences narrowed and eventually disappeared, yet the experience of rivalry in the early Republic left a discernible trace. Amid the bitterness of political warfare, fine distinctions of position were maintained. Striving to achieve a coherent and secure place in New England life, Republicans constituted a social group united by ties of kinship and marriage. The Austins, Townsends, and Gerrys intermarried, as did the Harrises azd Devenses of Charlestown; out in the Connecticut Valley marriage cemented ties between the families of William Lyman and Samuel Fowler. Eastern Republicans such as William Eustis and James Swan formed connections with the Langdons, New Hampshire's leading Jeffersonian family. The formation of Republican social connections was only one aspect of the processes by which aspiring elements united to further their interest.

[T]he Republican challenge had another dimension, which reached deeply into the hearts of the people and gave Bay State Jeffersonianism an emotional appeal that the contest for preferment hardly suggested. At the same time that men sought to enlarge opportunities in one sphere, they were questioning the legitimacy of power in another; just as they resisted secular authority they also opposed ecclesiastical establishment.

. . .Religious problems aroused men because they were local and personal, and because they stimulated disputation by many of the most articulate members of the community. The growing controversy over the establishment was important not only because of the substantive issues involved, but also because it gave parties a cause which cut across sectional, economic, and class lines. Advocacy of the separation of church and state gave Republicans a popular issue which appealed to large groups dissatisfied with the standing order and opened fresh possibilities of forging new links between the party and the people.

The spiritual life of the Commonwealth underwent important changes after independence. Congregationalism became weaker, dissent grew stronger, and problems of church and state were persistently troublesome. Each year after 1780 the establishment lost ground, and by the 1790's the instability in religious life propelled rival denominations into politics. The defenders of the standing order took refuge behind the Federalist banner while the forces of dissent rallied to the Republican standard. The debate between the two groups echoed the secular dialogue of the party politicians.

Because the outstanding and articulate figures among the clergy were Federalists, historians have generally viewed the ministry as monolithically committed to one party. Actually its loyalties were divided. The outspoken group whose sermons survived were not altogether typical of the great mass of pastors. Many Calvinists became Republicans because of their democratic social theory and their hostility to the liberal ideas of the Federalist elite on the seaboard. William Bentley, whose knowledge of religious life was extraordinary, noted that outside New England, Calvinists were generally Jeffersonians. He also believed that the Federal Calvinists in Massachusetts were not representative of Congregationalism. There were influential and articulate Jeffersonian Calvinists in the Bay State.

With visions of a millennial holocaust and a conspiracy of Illuminati, [established] Calvinists looked to Federalism to block the spread of Jacobinism, atheism, and their American exponents, the Democratic-Republicans. Through their "self-created" societies, their sympathy for French social changes, and their opposition to a religious establishment, Republicans marked themselves as enemies of order and the instruments of Illuminism.

Continuous controversy over church taxes and a series of unfavorable judicial decisions intensified dissatisfaction with the standing order and pushed the sects further into politics. Wherever dissent flourished, Republicans generally found political support. Though Hampshire and Worcester counties were heavily Federalist, the party showed strength in towns with Baptist concentrations. In Cheshire, the home of Elder John Leland, the highest vote the Federalists ever polled between 1800 and 1812 was seven out of a total of 241. Similarly, towns in Bristol and Plymouth counties and in the District of Maine [then a part of Massachusetts], where Baptists and Methodists were numerous, generally voted Republican. At the same time that a common antagonism to the establishment forged a political union of Calvinists and dissenters within the Republican party, these groups also found support from Jeffersonians, who shared neither their doctrines nor their grievances.

On this basis, Bay State Republicanism could unite rural Calvinists and urban rationalists, inland dissenters from the religious order and urban critics of the social order. It was through such processes that a diverse coalition of far-flung interests became a political party. Political change in the eastern maritime communities and the District of Maine further enlarged, broadened, and strengthened the Republican formation.

PARTY AND DIFFERENCE IN VIRGINIA

11   FROM   *Harry Ammon*
The Jeffersonian Republicans in Virginia

The problem of the origin and development of the Jeffersonian Republicans has long been of particular interest to historians. The realization that both the long prevailing agrarian-mercantile interpretation and the identification of the Republicans with the anti-federalists of 1788 are essentially over-simplifications has only served to deepen this interest. The title of the program on which this paper was originally presented—"The Jeffersonians; A Contrast, New York and Virginia," was in itself a recognition that the Republican Party, while bound together in the broad outlines of its national program, was not merely a national party, but one

SOURCE. Harry Ammon, "The Jeffersonian Republicans in Virginia: an Interpretation," *Virginia Magazine of History and Biograph,* LXXI (1963), pp. 153-155; 158-165. Reprinted by permission of Virginia Historical Society and the author.

which also had divergent origins and interests in the respective states. In order for this approach to be meaningfully illuminated in papers written independently and based upon research centering around two different states, Dr. Alfred Young and I agreed upon a set of questions, the answers to which would provide the "contrast" constituting the general theme of the session. . . .

The first question upon which we agreed—"Who were the Republicans?"—required some modification when posed in relation to the Old Dominion. In New York state with its richly diversified economic and social structure, embracing urban and rural elements, artisans and merchants, great landowners and yeoman farmers, this brief query opened up many roads for the analysis of both political behavior and party affiliations. However, in Virginia where we are confronted with an almost solid agrarian society that had no truly significant urban centers and where the merchant class was at once small and uninfluential, this question did not provide much basis for further investigation. It is true that the agrarian element in Virginia was diverse in wealth and status, but it presented that remarkable identity of interest and that sense of solidarity which has been so characteristic of the South as a whole. There was, to use an expression to which some may object, a monolithic quality about Virginia's social structure, not to be observed in New York. Thus, when we ask ourselves the general question as to who were the Virginia Republicans, the answer is simply the agrarian element, which in spite of its conclusiveness is not very illuminating. Closer examination of the Virginia scene reveals that the Federalists, by and large, also belonged to the very same class. It is true that Jefferson on occasion asserted that the Federalists were made up largely of merchants using British capital and Scotch traders, whose prevalence in the towns, particularly in Richmond, Norfolk, and Alexandria gave those places a Federalist tone. Yet this is patently a casual oversimplification with propaganda overtones, for some of the most important Federalists cannot be included in this category, e.g., Henry Lee, Francis Corbin, John Marshall, Patrick Henry (whose somewhat late and devious arrival to Federalism should perhaps disqualify him from this list), and finally that most distinguished of all Virginia Federalists, General George Washington. Certainly the Federalist convictions of Marshall (who had been an intimate friend of Monroe in the 1780's) perplexed his Republican contemporaries, for they had hoped for better things of him. James Madison (whether correctly or not) attributed Marshall's political affiliation to his involvement in the Fairfax land purchase and to his need for large loans from the Bank of the United States. Indeed, all the prominent Federalists were primarily associated with the landed gentry. Since this line of investigation belabors the obvious, it seems to me, that the unique features of Republicanism in Virginia can most effectively be highlighted if the question is rephrased to include the problem of the historical roots of the Republican movement.

Only when we ask to what extent did Republicanism (or for that matter Federalism) reflect the quarrels, factions, and habits of political action of the past do we enter a meaningful area of discussion. First, in Virginia—and here we have a significant contrast with both New York and Pennsylvania—the Republicans did not trace their movement in the slightest degree to any quarrel or faction prior to the conflict over the federal Constitution. The political life of the Old Dominion in the eighteenth century had been highly factional in character. That is, men were drawn together by their views on specific issues in the most ephemeral of alliances. Parties in the sense of continuing associations bound together by common goals or common principles (apart from the Revolutionary conflict) were totally unknown. After the Revolution, Virginians resumed their old habits, and the strong tradition of independent judgment shaped by a consideration of each measure in itself was fully restored. Thus neither party which emerged in the 1790's inherited any issues or allegiances from the past which could fundamentally affect its future membership or course of action. In this same era sectional differences were of no importance, for those difficulties which earlier in the century had chafed the relations between the Piedmont and the Tidewater had been largely settled. It was not until after 1800 that the rapid growth of the transmontane region reintroduced sectional conflicts to plague the political leaders of the nineteenth century.

The struggle over the ratification of the Constitution was an event of the utmost importance in the background of the formation of the first parties, but not, as is now well known, because there was any direct continuity between the anti-federalists and the Republicans nor between the federalists of 1788 and those of 1795. Although it is customary to refer to both the federalists and the anti-federalists of 1788 as "parties," this nomenclature, particularly as applied to Virginia, is inaccurate. A careful study of the conflict over the Constitution makes it abundantly clear that the federalists and anti-federalists were really factions in the customary Virginia style—i.e., two groups of men drawn together to achieve specific and limited objectives. . . .

The Jeffersonian Republicans were composed of both federalists and anti-federalists, and in this amalgam, at least during the 1790's those who had supported the ratification of the Constitution were the most conspicuous leaders of the party. Only one major figure in the higher echelon of party leadership—James Monroe—had been an anti-federalist, and as one of the leading advocates of a stronger government between 1783 and 1787 and as a close collaborator of Madison during these years, he cannot be numbered among the extremists. The Republicans were at first exclusively dominated by men with a nationalist point of view who had accepted the necessity of a government stronger than that provided by the Articles of Confederation. Yet, having been reared in a climate of opinion which placed enormous value on individual rights and stressed the evils of aristocratic privilege, they were by no means prepared to sacrifice personal liberty for governmental power. It was in the light of this heritage that both the friends and the enemies of the Constitution judged the conduct of the new government, and when they found it wanting, proceeded to organize a movement designed to put the government upon what they conceived to be its correct path.

The second question which must be considered in order to fully understand the Republican movement is that relating to the issues which gave rise to the first parties. The evolution of the Republican Party in Virginia can be traced in two distinct stages. First, the period of uneasiness experienced by most of the important political leaders in Virginia over the tendencies which Alexander Hamilton's program exhibited. They were not merely alarmed because it tended to favor the mercantile class, but also because it seemed a disguised method of creating a privileged class. Hamilton's operations seemed about to subvert the republican government which they approved into a monarchy. Unquestionably the known political opinions of the Secretary of the Treasury and his influence over the President contributed largely to these suspicions. This was the position in which the Republicans found themselves by the end of 1791 and which Thomas Jefferson so ably summarized in his well-known letter to Washington on May 23, 1792. It is not at all surprising that the Virginians with their emphasis upon individual rights and their preference for a government with strictly limited powers would have been concerned over what they could only interpret as determination to strengthen the federal government at the expense of constitutional restrictions. It was during this formative period that the first party lines were drawn, the first contacts established outside the state. The second phase did not begin until 1793 when the Republicans, who had up to this time acted as a rather loosely knit faction, rapidly coalesced into a distinct party under the impact of the controversy stirred up by the outbreak of war in Europe and by the radical turn of the French Revolution.

The heated conflicts which developed during the next few years centered about issues which were decisive in forging party lines. Many, such as Henry Lee and Francis Corbin, who had sympathized with the Jeffersonians in their criticism of the Hamiltonian system, now definitely entered the Federalist ranks, finding themselves unable to tolerate the approval given the Jacobins in France. Certainly the issue of the French Revolution played a much larger role in Republican propaganda than did the fiscal program of the government, for the attack on the financial system, as Monroe pointed out in 1792, was somewhat hampered by the inability of the Republicans to put forward counter proposals which would be any more palatable. Moreover, the French Revolution offered an issue which was more directly related in its implications to the traditional issues of liberty and freedom with which all Americans were fully familiar. It is most interesting to note that in 1793 both Jefferson and Madison, when seeking to determine political affiliation, made use of opinion about the French Revolution as a conclusive test. The French question and foreign affairs in general occupied a central position in Republican warfare on the administration until 1798 when the Federalists presented the opposition with the most ideal issue conceivable—the Alien and Sedition Acts. The possibility of using these measures to accomplish the rout of the Federalists was quickly realized and action was immediate. The Federalists in their panic had made it possible for the Republicans, who were deeply embarrassed by French policy at that time, to extricate themselves from an awkward`position. There is every indication that the Republicans were at that time seeking some new means of attacking their rivals, for Jefferson in 1797 was engaged in organizing a protest against a presentment of a Virginia federal grand jury which had condemned a circular letter sent by Republican Congressman Samuel J. Cabell to his constituents. Jefferson rightly saw this jury action as a violation of individual rights and an attempt to limit freedom of speech. Although he drafted a petition which was submitted to the General Assembly protesting the presentment, the more sensational nature of the Alien and Sedition Acts overshadowed this lesser, though similar, issue and no action was taken by the legislature.

In the formation of the Republican Party, we come now to the third and last question, which I will examine. . .namely, what was the Republican Party as an organized movement? This is an area which is still somewhat unfamiliar and deserves more extensive attention. In the modern sense party organization as such was completely unknown prior to the election of 1800. The few Democratic societies which sprang up in Virginia after the outbreak of the French Revolution were composed entirely of eager young men, who, apart from a few passionate addresses to the public, made no impact upon the political life of their time. Even the party press as a carefully nurtured and systematically directed organ of party opinion was in its primitive form of development. It is true that a considerable number of newspapers were established in Virginia during the 1790's, but none of these received the kind of support nor possessed the editorial direction to speak effectively for the party as a whole. Unquestionably Jefferson recognized the importance of the press, but until 1804 when Thomas Ritchie established the *Enquirer* and when we enter the age when the party was subjected to some sort of central discipline through the Richmond Junto, there was no dominant organ of party opinion.

The only organization which existed among the Virginia Republicans during the first decade of their activity was one completely within the limits of the political tradition of the Old Dominion—nothing more or less than an easy and informal association of like-minded gentlemen of large influence within the state. The only real difference between the 1790's and previous decades was that a new test for admission to the association of leaders was added to that of being a gentleman—namely, party affiliation. The demands of faction had not been as great as those of party, and in that simpler age before 1790 it had been possible for political leaders to shift from side to side on a given issue, or even remain uncommitted if they so desired, without risking political isolation. This pattern of aristocratic domination of politics, as the late Charles S. Sydnor has so brilliantly demonstrated in his *Gentlemen Freeholders* (Chapel Hill, 1952), not only characterized the political life of eighteenth-century Virginia but was perpetuated far into the nineteenth century. Although on the county level the number of families who were prominent in politics was relatively large, the real leadership in the colony and in the state was actually far more restricted and was by no means exclusively associated with family position. Prior to 1789 the political life of Virginia had centered around meetings of the legislature, which were the sole occasions during which the widely scattered local leaders were able to meet and formulate programs. It was during the sessions of the General Assembly that the alliances between politicians, brief as they were, sprang up. Not all the members of the legislature were equally important in determining the course of legislation, but the active and responsible direction of public affairs rested in the hands of a very few men— between a dozen and twenty. It was among these men that conflicts of opinion took place, and it was about them that factions were formed. . . .

Operating as they did within the basic pattern of colonial politics, the Republicans nonetheless made some adjustments required by the nature of party—after all a party, unlike a faction, must look to its future—and by the changed political circumstances resulting from the new [national] government. Perhaps one of the most important alterations was the new attitude to elections. In the past, elections had been largely conducted by local figures without any outside intervention. By and large they had been popularity contests in which issues had been distinctly secondary. This could no longer be permitted. The candidates still had to possess a suitable social standing in order to insure their approval by the local gentry, but now they must also be clearly identified by the voter as belonging to one political party or the other. It was equally necessary that the voter be made aware of this new criterion in exercising his franchise. The realization of this goal was by no means easy, since it was a radical departure from past habits. Even as late as 1795 we find Madison complaining that only in two districts had the Congressional elections turned upon (as he put it) "*political* rather than *personal* considerations." Hence it was always possible that a Federalist gentleman of enormous local popularity could win in a normally Republican county unless the voters realized that being a Federalist must bar him permanently from their affections. Undoubtedly this problem was one of the considerations leading to the adoption of the general electoral ticket in 1799—to clearly identify the individual with the party.

The Republican control of the legislature from the very earliest stages of their formation enabled that party to make use of the General Assembly to mobilize public opinion against the measures of the Washington Administrations. Starting with the session of 1790-1791 when [Patrick] Henry's strongly worded resolutions attacking the assumption of the state debts were adopted, nearly every session during the next decade saw the passage of resolutions designed to affect public opinion. Such legislative expressions were by no means new, but in the past they had been distinctly expressions of the will of the state and not party pronouncements designed to have some effect upon opinion either in Virginia or in the other states. Useful as these legislative resolutions were, occasions arose which required more direct action. It was now of prime importance that the electorate be informed of the stand taken by the party, and hence it was no longer possible to suspend political action until the annual session of the General Assembly. To fill this need the Republicans had recourse to the public meeting of citizens which had played such a useful role in arousing the public at the time of the conflict with England. Curiously enough this device was revived by the Federalists, although subsequently monopolized by the Republicans. In August 1793 the Federalists (who never had a chance to use the legislature) organized meetings in Richmond, Norfolk, and Winchester for the purpose of endorsing Washington's foreign policy. The Republicans were not only surprised by this tactical maneuver, but pained that the Richmond meeting should have been presided over by George Wythe, whom they numbered among their ranks. Quickly recovering from their surprise Monroe and Madison with Jefferson's approval organized a series of counter-meetings to bring out, as Madison put it with unintentional irony, the real sense of the people on the President's proclamation. Model sets of resolutions were dispatched to their influential friends throughout the state with the suggestion that they be varied somewhat to give the appearance of spontaneity. It goes without saying that the Republicans on this as on other occasions were able to overwhelm the opposition by the greater number of their meetings. The public meeting continued to be a regular feature of political activity prior to 1800. The last massive use of meetings was in connection with the Alien and Sedition Acts. After the turn of the century they became less frequent, being rendered less necessary by the decline of party warfare and by the formation of a more effectively controlled party press.

At the very end of the decade, an entirely new feature was introduced into the existing party structure—the legislative caucus. The first Virginia caucus about which we know in detail was that which met in 1800 for the purpose of selecting presidential electors and to nominate members of a central corresponding committee and subordinate county committees to manage the campaign. For the first time in the history of the party official agencies were established, although of strictly limited powers and confined exclusively to the period prior to the election. In the future caucuses were to become a regular feature of party activity. This development preserved the legislature as the center of political activity and leadership within the state. The final evolution in party machinery did not take place until Jefferson retired from the presidency, when the so-called "Richmond Junto" emerged to assume a controlling interest over party affairs. The Junto was by no means a radical departure from the past—its members were drawn from the upper class group and most (though not all) of its members had seats in the legislature. However, it did lead to certain ossification in the political framework of Virginia. It tended to be dominated by those of its members who either lived in or very close to Richmond and hence could be available for conferences at times when the legislature was not in session. It tended to be less flexible in opening its ranks to new members and developed a pronounced insularity in both national and state politics. Thus, for example, it favored the eastern banking interests established in Richmond and ignored the demands of the western portion of the state for more extensive banking facilities.

In this paper I have tended to stress the continuity of the Republicans with the past—not in party organization as such—but in the perpetuation of the political habits of the Colonial era and the enduring effect of the ideological framework of the Revolution. I have made no mention of local conflicts or issues in connection with the formation of the Republican party simply because there were none at all. During the 1790's there was not a single issue in state politics which led to a conflict between the Federalists and the Republicans. Both of these aspects are of extreme importance, I think, because they placed the Republican leaders of Virginia in a unique position in relation to all the party leaders in the other states. Untroubled by any internal conflicts within the party and faced by an opposition which steadily grew more feeble, the party leaders of Virginia could and did devote themselves exclusively to national concerns. At no time did a purely local issue distract the Virginians from their preoccupation with the affairs of the nation. So secure were most of the Virginians in their positions of leadership within the state that it was rarely necessary for them to rush home to engage in extensive fence mending in their districts. . . .

It may be wondered if the world of the Virginia Republicans was such an ideal Arcadia in which large and small farmers alike were united in conviction and interest. Was this sense of tranquillity so idyllic that it was never shattered? Never even questioned? On the whole this seems to have been the case. The enormous sense of solidarity between all farmers, this acceptance of upper-class leadership, which was so deeply rooted in the traditions of the past, continued undisturbed until well into the nineteenth century. This state of affairs cannot be attributed to the dead hand of the past nor to the apathy of the lesser farmers, but rather it endured because it met the approval of all classes who consciously worked at making it a reality. Although we frequently talk rather glibly of upper-class or aristocratic domination of Virginia politics, it must never be forgotten that this control was not based upon privilege but upon elections. The power of the gentry rested upon the consent of the voter, and no matter how wealthy or prominent a man might be, he could lose an election as did George Washington in 1755. Gentle birth was a qualification for office, but not a guarantee of political preferment.

STILL-FEDERALIST
DELAWARE

12   FROM   *John A. Munroe*
Federalist Delaware 1775-1815

In the 1790s the Delaware Federalists ran state affairs in their own way. Political offices were revolved among a group of leaders. George Read began the decade as a United States Senator and left that position to become chief justice, after having been offered his choice of judicial posts by Governor Joshua Clayton. Until his death in 1798, Read appears to have relinquished little of his political leadership; Clayton consulted him regarding judicial and senatorial appointments, and in 1796 it was Read's brother-in-law, Gunning Bedford, Sr., who succeeded Clayton as governor. . . .

A regular practice of advancement from Representative to Senator seems to have been followed by the Delaware Federalists,

SOURCE. John A. Munroe, *Federalist Delaware 1775-1815,* pp. 198-208 (New Brunswick: Rutgers University Press, 1954).

for it fell to the lot of every Federalist Representative from Delaware in this decade—John Vining, Henry Latimer, and James A. Bayard—to move directly or indirectly from the lower house of Congress to the upper. By reason of Delaware's equal representation in spite of its small size, a Senator occupied the most important position it was in the power of the state to grant.

Among the Delaware Federalists, and their opponents too, family connections played such an important part that the Delaware historian must be something of a genealogist. Dare he neglect, for instance, to note that Senator William Hill Wells was the son-in-law of General John Dagworthy, or that Senator John Wales had a similar relationship to Representative John Patten, and Senator James A. Bayard to Senator Richard Bassett? The number of inter-family relationships among the political leaders of Delaware is truly astonishing.

At the beginning of the 1790s party alignments were not well established. Religious affiliations and attitudes toward the Revolution were overshadowed by the more important factor of desire for office and for whatever power, prestige, and profits its attainment might make possible; it was an eternal striving of "outs" against "ins," of the "have-nots" of state jobs against the "haves." As time passed, however, the European wars and questions of national policy caused increasing discussion and resulted by the end of the century, in the gradual emergence of two contesting parties. "Let the people be no longer amused, with the idle and useless distinctions of *Whig* and *Troy, court party* and *country party, presbyterian* and *church, aristocrat* and *democrat*; they neither apply to time nor place; but let them take up the only true and useful distinction, of *federal* and *anti-federal*, of *friends* to their *country* and *enemies* to *it.*." So, in 1794, a Federalist explained party differences.

Divided opinion on Jay's negotiation of a treaty with Britain gave impetus to the development of a party which opposed the dominant faction in Delaware. In spite of the treaty's unpopularity in the state and in the nation, the General Assembly passed a resolution commending the action of the President and the Senate in approving the treaty. Disapproval of the Assembly's action was registered in the unanimous resolution of a town meeting held in Wilmington at the Presbyterian church (the choice of meeting place was not without certain significance). With Dr. Tilton in the chair and Robert Coram acting as secretary, the eloquent young Democrat, Caesar A. Rodney, and John Dickinson, whom Rodney introduced as "a venerable Patriot. . .grown grey in the faithful discharge of his duties in the legislative, Judicial and Executive departments of government," spoke in opposition to the treaty. Rodney opposed any treaty with a nation as warlike as Britain, especially when it was fighting the French Republic. Dickinson spoke for two hours, "his Voice feble," until Thomas Rodney, having already heard his beloved son, "got wary and left the meeting." A more riotous group assembled at Christiana Bridge, where John Jay and the Delaware Senators, John Vining and Henry Latimer, who had favored the treaty, were denounced and burned in effigy.

There is evidence, from a reference made publicly, that those in Delaware directing this expression of opposition to Jay's Treaty were well acquainted with public protests against it made elsewhere in the union. Further evidence of a close relationship with national political developments is furnished by the establishment, a year before the treaty was signed, of a society apparently formed on the order of the famous Democratic Society of Philadelphia. On June 14, 1794, notice was given in a Wilmington newspaper that 'At a respectable Meeting of Citizens of New Castle County in the town of Newcastle, it was unanimously agreed to form themselves into a political Society." A committee was named which submitted a constitution and a declaration of principles to the next meeting of the group, henceforth to be known as the "Patriotic Society of Newcastle County, in the State of Delaware."

The group which dominated the Patriotic Society was also in control of the Society of the Cincinnati, whose chief officers in 1794 were John Patten, first Republican Congressman from Delaware, and Peter Jaquett and William McKennan, both members of the Patriotic Society. On July 4, 1794, the Cincinnati toasted the French Republic, and two years later they also drank to "the patriots of Ireland," equality, and "the extinction of Monarchy in essence as well as in name." Clearly the Delaware Cincinnati were full of Republican spirit.

The growing opposition to Federal rule is also demonstrated by the organization of independent military companies in New Castle County in 1794. William McKennan was the colonel of these volunteers, who objected to Governor Clayton's appointments to offices in the militia; refusing to fight except under officers of their own choice, these men were consequently being called before a justice of the peace as "militia delinquents." "A Ci-Devant Refugee," probably a Federalist in disguise, suspected that there were "emissaries among them from the Western insurgents" of the Whiskey Rebellion, that their dissatisfaction with the militia law was a mere blind, and that their intent was "to effect an entire subversion of the government." In August the Wilmington Independent Volunteer Company was ordered to parade in full uniform to New Castle to "join the Political Society for Constitutional Information" (*i.e.*, the Patriotic Society), a proceeding which "One of the People" condemned as an attempt to infuse the volunteers with the spirit of party. "An artificial volcano is prepared," he claimed, "composed of *political, national and religious principles* and *prejudices* of every king."

The reference to religious prejudice meant, of course, the rivalry between Presbyterians and Episcopalians. "Gracchus," a Republican, declared in 1794 that for nine years no Presbyterian had been sent to the legislature from Kent County, where in 1792 magistrates and judges had urged the people not to elect a Presbyterian, especially "an *Irish* presbyterian just *imported.*" The "volcano" of "principles and prejudices" in dissent with the ruling faction had finally been given a name by January, 1795, when the notice of a meeting of "the Social Club" solicited "the attendance of every Democratic Republican, whose heart is susceptible of the Social Converse."

While the conservative faction continued to win most of the elections and therefore to dominate Delaware politics through this period of the formation of parties, its control was effectively challenged in the middle of the decade when John Patten was sent to Congress. As a matter of fact, Patten was twice the choice of a majority of Delawareans for Congress before he was permitted to serve a full term. In 1792 he contested the election with Henry Latimer, a physician and member of a prominent mercantile family, and was declared elected by President Clayton. Latimer, however, protested to the House of Representatives after Patten had already been seated.

The significance of this contest is greater than it might at first glance seem. For Latimer, who supported Army and Navy appropriations and all revenue bills, was clearly a Federalist, while Patten was a leader of the country party in Kent, which, at this very time, was becoming part of the new Democratic-Republican party. "Veritas," a Federalist, declared that Patten "threw himself into the arms of the Virginia party, who seemed to wish to involve the country in a precipitate war," while Latimer "uniformly supported the federal measures, which were ultimately adopted by the majority of Congress, sanctioned by the President, and. . .approved by the cooler judgment of the people of the United States."

Patten and his brothers-in-law, Joseph and Edward Miller in Kent, along with David Hall and Joseph Haslet in Sussex and Caesar A. Rodney, James Tilton, Robert Coram, and Hezekiah Niles (who was later to win fame through his weekly) in New Castle, were among the group which plotted to overthrow the political hierarchy of Delaware. Little is heard of the Patriotic Society after it published in 1795 an address, probably written by Rodney, Coram, and Tilton, defending popular societies against attack, especially on the basis of their being "self-created." The *Delaware Gazette,* however, remained the organ of the new party through most of this decade.

In 1795 the Federalists sought to rescue themselves "from those factions which prevail, & which are so enemical to the peace order & dignity of government" by choosing delegates from each county to meet at Dover and nominate a candidate for governor. Gunning Bedford, Sr., army veteran and brother-in-law of George Read, was their choice; Dr. Archibald Alexander, a retired army surgeon from Virginia who now lived near New Castle, was the candidate of the Democrats. A member of the latter party declared that it opposed not the government but the men in it, that it stood for France and republicanism, while the Federalists, the "aristocratic party," stood for Britain and monarchy.

The contest was hard fought. "Electioneering," said John Fisher, "was probably never at such an height in the county of Kent before. Bets run very high." "Tom Berry, one of the country candidates, roasted a steer and an half dozen of Sheep. . .as a kind of snack for his friends." A candidate in St. Georges Hundred gave a "fish-feast," and a "turtle-feast" was held at New Castle. At least three vessels were available to carry the voters from Wilmington to the county seat. "The United States are now divided into two parties," a Federalist handbill declared; of the local candidates, Bedford was "an old and tried friend of his country" and a supporter of Washington, while Alexander was "a partizan of Tilton and Genet." Bedford won the election, but Alexander carried New Castle, the home county of both candidates.

Federalist triumphs continued through the concluding years of the century. Patten refused to run for reelection to Congress in 1796 and was succeeded by the Federalist, James A. Bayard, the Democratic candidate being William Peery, of Sussex. In 1798 Bayard was returned to Congress, his father-in-law, Bassett, chosen governor, and a legislature elected which completed the Federalist triumph by sending William Hill Wells to the Senate. "The Federalists," a friend wrote Wells, are "Universally rejoicing in your election. . . .I have often bless'd my Stars that not one d—n democrat voted for you."

The Democrats, building on the strength of the old country party, found their greatest support in New Castle County, where the Scotch-Irish Presbyterian population was largest. "The Friends of Wilmington," Nathaniel Luff declared, were also "generally-. . .ranked in the political scale as favourable to Democracy." Though difficulties with France lent popularity to the Federalist cause in 1798, allowing Bassett to carry every county, the Democrats gradually won control of New Castle County. Kent County, however, became definitely Federalist and "this with the ordinary superiority" of that party in Sussex counteracted "the democratical fetes of N. Castle County."

In the bitter election of 1800, the Democrats made a valiant effort to carry Delaware. John Patten was brought from political retirement to run for Congress in the hope that his Revolutionary War record would garner the necessary independent votes for his party. The Jeffersonians attacked Bayard, the incumbent, and the Federalists in general for supporting the Alien and Sedition Acts, the quasi-war with France, taxes for the Army and Navy, and opposition to the Chesapeake and Delaware Canal. They sang "A New Republican Song":

> *Ye Farmers, Mechanics, Republicans all,*
> *Who would rescue your rights from*

unjust usurpation,
Resort to Newcastle at Liberty's call,
And unite all your votes with the
Voice of the Nation.

The Federalists also conducted a vigorous campaign. Allen McLane, Revolutionary hero and Wilmington port collector, was reported by the *Mirror* to have been sent to Kent, where he had formerly lived, on an electioneering tour to persuade the people that the Jacobinical Democrats would if victorious "drown all the men, women, and children in Kent and Sussex." These two counties remained loyal to Bayard and his party, which was victorious in spite of the opposition in New Castle.

PART FOUR
New Men in Power

A sharp reversal in party fortunes came with the national elections of 1800. Previously dominant Federalists succumbed to a Republican ascendency that was to last for years. It was also the first time in history that an extended nation had effected a peaceful transfer of power by democratic means.

Most states made their presidential choice by way of their legislatures, with only five of 16 states naming electors by popular vote. Even so, excitement reached new peaks, as voters went to the polls to choose the legislators who would name the electors. Especially hard-fought campaigns were waged in New York, Pennsylvania, and South Carolina, the crucial battlegrounds that ultimately gave the Republicans their edge. Across the land, an active band of partisan and often virulent newspapers trumpeted the virtues of their candidate and the evils of his opponent. The results were close: Thomas Jefferson had 73 electoral votes to 65 for John Adams. When it developed that Jefferson and Aaron Burr, his vice-presidential running mate, had the same number of electoral votes, it required 36 ballots in the House of Representatives to confirm Jefferson's election. He took office on time, however, and he was to make the most of it.

The Republican tide was better exemplified by the congressional results. In the outgoing Congress there were 19 Federalists to 13 Republicans in the Senate, and 64 Federalists to 42 Republicans in the House. After the elections of 1800, the balance was 18 Republicans to 14 Federalists in the Senate, and 69 Republicans to 36 Federalists in the House, almost a two-to-one margin. Every two years until the bitter Embargo election of 1808, moreover, the Republicans added to their majorities in both chambers. Te party of Washington and Hamilton was never to elect another president or to hold a majority in either house of Congress. It experienced brief revivals after 1808 and at the onset of the War of 1812.

Otherwise it fell back on its bastions in Massachusetts, Connecticut, and Delaware, and on local enclaves in a few other states. The Jeffersonians celebrated their "Revolution of 1800" for years to come. Yet, as Noble E. Cunningham points out, these "celebrations" were also "party appeals." The Republicans also worked to strengthen and extend the remarkable, earlier-day organization they had built up for the campaign of 1800. As a self-consciously "popular," modern political party, they undertook a broad, continuing mobilization of the voters.

Contrary to older interpretations, however, a hardy band of Federalists fought back. Stalwart partisans whom David Hackett Fischer calls "Young Federalists," as contrasted with the "Old Federalists" who had founded the party, strove to turn Jeffersonian techniques against their inventors. Deference patterns, political subordination to social superiors or elites, were beginning to give way to more independent attitudes, although the decline of deference was painfully slow in many areas. A fresh approach to the electorate was essential if the Federalists ever hoped to regain power. The answer, according to the Federalist young men, was to use popular political methods in order to shore up the old cause of fundamentally elitist goals. In short, as Fischer notes, the "Young Federalists" sought to turn "the forms of democracy against its substance." Even so, many old Federalists bitterly resisted any attempts toward overt popular appeals, or indeed any modernization of the party; and others gave up in disgust. In the end, the younger Federalists failed. Their efforts were too little and, mostly, too late to save the party or the cause.

As Jefferson took office in 1801, John Marshall remarked that he would seek "to embody himself with the House"—in effect, act as a guiding spirit in the new Republican Congress. Indeed, Jefferson exerted executive leadership accordingly. In some measure he did so as a party leader; but in some degree his endeavor was personal and depended on his unique prestige and persuasiveness. The Republicans created a remarkable record, fulfilling many of the policy objectives that they had proclaimed while they were out of power. Events took them further, however, as Noble E. Cunningham shows again. When Jefferson tried to go beyond the Louisiana Purchase of 1803 and get funds from Congress to buy Spanish Florida too, a party rupture ensued. It was led by John Randolph, the ers-while informal Republican leader in the House: the position of majority leader as we know it today was well in the future. To replace the erratic Randolph with a reliable spokesman, Jefferson first called on Caesar A. Rodney of Delaware; when Rodney was defeated for reelection, Jefferson sought out Barnabas Bidwell of Massachusetts; and when Bidwell withdrew to pursue his political career in the Bay State, the President finally turned to Wilson Cary Nicholas of Virginia. It was not easy, trying to recruit so many congressional managers in so few years. But Jefferson knew the import of the job, and persisted in the quest.

In his executive role, Jefferson often moved in a decisive and even hard-boiled fashion to serve partisan purposes. He was no conscienceless spoilsman in the manner of the late nineteenth century, but he knew the importance of patronage for building party strength. In contrast to older treatments that have stressed Jefferson's careful "moderation" in appointments and removals, Carl A. Prince maintains that he was quite ready to follow a policy of "sweeping political removal." Confronted with an entrenched, Federalist "social and political aristocracy," Prince argues, the Republican President was determined to cut out its roots of power in the federal bureaucracy. So it was with the problem of Federalist holdovers in the court system, from judges to marshals; and so it was with other positions, such as revenue officers and the customs service. In the process, the President as party leader was particularly industrious in removing active, "Young Federalists" from the positions they held.

The result was that Jefferson not only enhanced Republican strength, but he made it still harder for the second generation of Federalists to pursue their belated efforts to renovate their party.

PARTIES AND THE VOTER

13   FROM   *Noble E. Cunningham, Jr.*
The Republican Appeal

That Republican leaders sought to encourage a feeling of popular participation in the affairs of the party and to keep alive popular enthusiasm for the party was well demonstrated by the frequency of party celebrations held throughout the country. Many of the Republican celebrations which accompanied the inauguration of Jefferson on March 4, 1801, were well-planned, elaborate demonstrations which featured parades, dinners, orations, balls, and other festivities. These celebrations were repeated in many places in March of each year throughout Jefferson's administration. "The 4th of March forms an epoch in the political history of the United States, which ought always to awaken the purest sensations of the American Patriot," declared a Richmond Republican meeting in announcing "the celebration of that day, which restored to us the genuine principles of '76, and removed the alarms which had clouded the fairest prospects of American

SOURCE. Noble E. Cunningham, Jr., *The Jeffersonian Republicans in Power: Party Operations, 1801-1809*, pp. 284-289 (Chapel Hill: University of North Carolina Press, 1963). Reprinted by permission of the publisher, the Institute of Early American History and Culture, and the author.

Liberty and Independence." Reporting the Republican celebration in New Haven in March 1803, Abraham Bishop enthusiastically pointed out that "the procession extended in close columns through two sides of the public square and consisted of 1108 men. The whole company far exceeded that on commencements and Elections." The Boston *Independent Chronicle* on Monday, March 5, 1804, announced: "This Day, the anniversary of the renovation of *Republicanism* in the United States, in the inauguration of the patriot, the sage, the inflexible Republican, will be celebrated in the most splendid manner."

In addition to the March 4th celebrations, there were also the July 4th festivities which came to be separately observed by the two parties in many places. A July 4th celebration planned and controlled by Republicans meant, as explained by Levi Lincoln, "a republican orator, republican prayers, republican music, republican toasts, and republican songs." Special celebrations were also held, the most elaborate and extensive being the celebration of the acquisition of Louisiana. From Washington, Federalist Congressman Manasseh Cutler reported in January 1804: "There is a *Jubilee* proclaimed here by the Democrats. . . .There is to be such a feast, it is said, as was never known in America, on account of taking possession of *Louisiana*. There is to be dinners—suppers—balls—assemblies, dances, and I know not what. . . .The *Jubilee* is to begin here—but they expect it will run—like *wildfire*, to every dark and benighted corner of America." And spread it did. Republican newspapers called for a national festival, and Republicans in many parts of the country organized celebrations. So tremendous was the Philadelphia celebration that it must have dominated the life of the city for days, even weeks, before the May 12 festival.

Federalists replied to the Republican celebrations by observing Washington's birthday, just before the March 4th festivals, and in other ways calling attention to the first President. The Worcester *Massachusetts Spy*, obviously trying to counteract recent Republican demonstrations, devoted most of the issue of March 7, 1804, to publishing Washington's Farewell Address.

Although every election had its own peculiar set of circumstances and many voters were influenced in their suffrages by considerations often of a local or personal nature, there were certain appeals voiced sufficiently frequently and universally by Republican candidates and party spokesmen that they may be correctly referred to as party appeals. These Republican appeals reveal the issues or lack of issues which were presented to the voters, as well as the methods by which party workers sought to advance the Republican cause.

First of all, the Republicans who had successfully turned out John Adams in 1800 campaigned against Adams as long as they could keep alive the memories of the unpopular measures of his administration. A circular in support of Republican candidates for the legislature of Maryland in September 1802 declared:

"Sir, you cannot have forgotten the unjust and oppressive measures of the late administration.

"WHO imposed, unnecessarily, upon the people a debt of upwards of ten millions?—The Federalists.

"WHO laid and continued the tax on your stills?—The Federalists.

"WHO taxed your dwelling houses?—The Federalists.

"WHO taxed your lands?—The Federalists.

"WHO imposed on you a Stamp-Act, and created an *host of officers* to collect the excise duties?—The Federalists.

"WHO imposed on you an alien law, a Sedition Act, and a new and unnecessary Judiciary law. . .?—The Federalists.

"WHO raised a useless standing army?—The Federalists. . . .

"The *principal* actors in the Federal measures approve of the former, and are dissatisfied with the present administration. . . .

"The question before you is, do you wish those measures of extravagant Taxation pursued by the Federalists re-established?"

Republican delegates from the various counties of New Jersey in recommending the Republican ticket for Congress in 1803 explained: "It is not necessary. . .to recall to the recollection of their fellow-citizens, the extravagant, oppressive, and unconstitutional measures of the late administration; or to direct their attention to the economical, pacific, and equitable conduct of the present. Every friend to a republican government, in form and substance, must wish to avert a recurrence of the scenes that marked Mr. Adams's administration, and to perpetuate the system practised by the administration of Mr. Jefferson." The Democratic Republican Corresponding Committee of New-Castle County, Delaware, in 1804, announced that "the Committee would be willing to rest the fate of the approaching general election in the State of Delaware on the comparative review. . .of the measures and policy of the *former* and *present* administrations, believing that the public suffrages will give a decided preference to the friends of the *latter* who are candidates for office—and this on the score of economy alone, if there were no other reasons." The Democratic Republicans of Gloucester County, New Jersey, in 1807, authorized the printing and distribution of five hundred copies of an address, "containing a brief narrative of the most oppressive laws passed during the federal administration, their extravagant expenditure of the public money, prosecutions, fines and imprisonments, to prevent freedom of speech, or an investigation of their conduct; contrasted with the conduct of the present administration."

In the election of 1808, when the Federalists, hoping to take advantage of the unpopularity of the Embargo, made their strongest efforts thus far to regain popular support, the issues of the Adams administration were revived with increased vigor. A Republican reply to William Gaston, who was running as a Federalist elector in support of Charles Cotesworth Pinckney in North Carolina, concluded:

"General Pinckney, as to political principles, is just such a man, Fellow-Citizens, as you dismissed from office eight years ago, on account of those principles. If you elect Mr. Gaston, he will endeavor to give you a Federal President. If this should take place, it is reasonable to conclude, that under similar circumstances, he would act as the former President did. Therefore. . .you must expect—"Alien and Sedition Laws—Direct,—Stamp,—Still and other Internal TAXES."

A notice printed in Republican newspapers called attention to the difference between the Adams and Jefferson administrations in the following comparison:

LOOK ON

THIS PICTURE	AND ON THIS

During *four* years of Adams' administration the National Debt was *augmented* eleven millions of dollars; a host of judges appointed to receive large salaries and carry the sedition law, etc., into execution, and so intimidate a free people; four hundred tax-gatherers were employed to collect the internal direct taxes on lands, houses, stills, carriages, sugar, and domestic distilled spirits. Navies were built, armies were raised; and loans were obtained at the enormous interest of eight per cent—to maintain the system of direful waste and extravagance.

During Jefferson's republican administration, the *whole system* of internal taxes has been abolished; the superfluous and useless judges dismissed; and even the duties on imports in some cases diminished. No tax is paid to the general government; —yet near 30 *millions* of the public debt has been redeemed; and Louisiana purchased for *fifteen* millions of dollars— though it is worth sixty millions of dollars, renders us secure on the S.W. border of the Union, and produces cotton and sugar in great abundance. And of the 15 millions, three went to compensate our own merchants for spoliations.

The preceding illustrations not only indicate how Republicans throughout the country campaigned against the previous administration, but they also show how Republicans in both national and state elections stood on the record of the administration. Printed circular letters sent by Republican congressmen to their constituents also were filled with glowing praise of the accomplishments of the administration which they supported and which they pledged themselves to continue to support if re-elected.

14 FROM *David Hackett Fischer*
The Federalist Counter-Effort

We have a new set of leader. . . .Let us have men who can relax
their principles of morality as occasion may require and adapt
themselves to circumstances.

WILLIAM PLUMER, 1803

The defeat of such Federalists as John Jay [in New York] and
George Cabot [in Massachusetts] did not mark the death of
Federalism. As the gentlemen of the old school were making a
rather ungentlemanly departure from public life, another group of
Federalist leaders began to replace them—a fresh generation of
dynamic young men who brought new life to a lost cause, new
strength to the shattered enterprises of the old school.

Together, of course, these two generations of American conservatives shared more than merely a party name. Both were elitists in
their social attitudes; both agreed that "men of talents should
give, not receive direction from the multitude." Both tended to
identify talents and virtue with birth and breeding, with blood
and wealth, with beauty and refinement in dress, demeanor, and
physical appearance.

But if elitist purposes remained constant, electoral practices did
not. In the midst of many changes, the younger Federalists moved
uncertainly toward new patterns of political behavior which
contrasted sharply with the precepts of the old school. The
contrast between the two generations of American conservatives
was itself a measure of change in the political structure of the new
republic.

SOURCE. David Hackett Fischer, *The Revolution of American Conservatism: The
Federalist Party in the Era of Jeffersonian Democracy,* pp. 29-35, 91, 93, 95-7, 99-102, 105-
7, 109 (New York: Harper and Row, 1965). Copyright c 1965 by David Hackett
Fischer. Reprinted by permission of Harper & Row, Publishers, Inc.

Born between 1760 and 1789, the second generation of Federalists matured in an "age of convulsions and overturning," a period in which, as John Quincy Adams observed, change itself appeared to be the only constant. Not least among these many changes in America was an alteration in the relationship between gentlemen and politics. Federal gentlemen of the old school were products of a society which had expected and even required men of wealth and reputation to take leading parts in the affairs of the commonwealth. Public office was at once an eighteenth-century gentleman's sacred right, his special property, and his saving obligation.

But by the century's end a perceptible gap was opening between politics and people "of the better sort." An important study, "The American Business Elite," by a history-minded sociologist, C. Wright Mills, offers striking evidence of political disengagement by men of property in the generation of the young Federalists. . . .In the generation of the old-school Federalists, 71 per cent of Mills's business leaders held public office, a figure near to that for earlier age-groups. But in the generation of the young Federalists, participation in public affairs dropped suddenly to 46 per cent and continued to fall very slowly thereafter.

This startling change might be explained in several ways. Perhaps men of wealth were being driven out of politics by other men who practiced the arts of popular politics with greater freedom, power, and effect. This was the view of a British traveler in the new nation. "The leading Federalists," he wrote, "are gentlemen of fortune, talents and education, the natural leaders of the country. The leaders of the democratic party, on the other hand, are for the most part, what may be called politicians of fortune; adventurers who follow politics as a profession. With them politics are a pecuniary, with the Federalists, they are a secondary consideration. The democrats being men of inferior birth and breeding to the Federalists, can more easily mix with the rabble, and practice the tribunitian arts. They affect, with their dress and manners, to regard themselves as of the Plebian order, and condescend to a familiarity of intercourse with the vulgar from which gentlemen would revolt."

Whatever the explanation, the brute fact of a bifurcation between politics and propriety. . .is clear, in this and other evidence. Changing attitudes and assumptions appeared in the

changing connotation of words such as "politics" and "politician."
Before 1800 both appear to have been neutral in themselves,
Hamilton in *The Federalist Papers,* for example, spoke of "the little
arts of the little politician" at one point, and of "wise politicians"
at another. After 1800, however, both words usually bore negative
connotations. Fisher Ames wrote of his "pigsty and politics, two
scurvy subjects that should be coupled together." Timothy Pickering equated "the *public cheat"* with "the *politician."* This usage was
not limited merely to disgruntled Federalists. In 1812 a Republican explained, "what I mean by *politics* are those petty topics of
ribaldry and abuse which *newspaper-readers* are continually bab-
bling about." John Randolph of Roanoke spoke bitterly of "the
refuse of the retail trade of politics." And a lady of no particular
persuasion disturbed Mrs. John Quincy Adams by observing that
her son "is formed for a politician; he understands the art of
twisting a subject better than any child she ever saw."

With the decline of deference, politics itself had become a dirty
business, in the judgment of the "better sort of people," a low
trade from which neither honor nor reputation could be gained.
Gentlemen of the old school, who had been educated to regard
public affairs as their private responsibility, advised their sons
after 1800 to keep clear. The fastidious needed no urging. The
North Carolina Federalist who, in 1803, repudiated a nomination
because he was "unwilling to make enemies and have my character bandied about through so many counties," personifies a
prejudice which has pervaded American society from his time to
ours.

The younger Federalists who became active in public affairs
after 1800 faced a double-ended dilemma. They meant to preserve
as much of the elitism of early American society as possible, but in
a new Republican context in which the "multitude" were being
invited to participate more actively, more meaningfully in politics,
and in which their "natural leaders" were turning to private
affairs. Younger Federalists nourished a traditional respect for
"orders and distinctions" in society, but ancient axioms of the old
school, time-honored techniques of political management, were
reduced to mere irrelevacies.

In the midst of conflict and discontinuities of so many kinds,
many members of the new generation of Federalism undertook a

new experiment in elitist politics—endeavoring to turn the forms of democracy against its substance, to combine the rhetoric of popular government with the hard reality of the iron law of oligarchy. In place of the happy vision of a silent multitude and a speaking elite, they substituted an uglier but more workable arrangement—a silent elite in the midst of a speaking multitude. "You must get close to the people in order to manage them," a young Federalist candidly declared; "there is no better way."

The shield and weapon of Federalism in the political arena, the engine of its new-modeled elitism, the essential political artifact, was party. Young Federalists who actively supported the cause positively defended the partisan spirit which united them, even if it divided the nation. They condoned otherwise indefensible tactics as necessary for "the good of the party." They preached submission to party discipline as a cardinal virtue of politics. "It is manifest," one of them wrote, "that the politician is bound to support the principles of his party, and not to represent his own opinion."

Young Federalists could find comfort and assurance in a biblical injunction. "Unto the pure all things are pure," Paul had written. They were bound together in a cause which in its righteousness served to sanctify the most ignoble means. The good of the cause itself became the measure of morality. "As a party we stand on the most elevated ground," wrote Alexander Contee Hanson in the midst of one of the most squalid political campaigns in the history of the state. "Besides justice, honor and everything else that can recommend a cause Providence seems to be on our side." Psychic identity was extraordinarily complete. In 1817, when Hanson learned of an internecine quarrel which promised to disrupt the Federal organization in Maryland, he wrote, "I tremble for the party. When the news first came, I felt exactly as if I saw one of my children on the eave of a high house hanging on by the nails."

Federalists spoke of the federal party as the "spartan band" which stood militantly between civilization and barbarism. It is psychologically significant to note that a military metaphor was characteristic. No sense of social harmony, such as had appeared in the mellower notions of the old school, manifested itself in the social and political thought of younger Federalists. To the class consciousness of the old school, younger men added a new sense of class conflict. The world was returned to a Hobbesian state of nature—a state of selfishness and strife, of turmoil and trouble. The political world became a battlefield. The other party was the enemy, and a no man's land lay in between. . . .

If the very name Federalist could not be cleansed, then in the interest of the new *sub rosa* elitism, it too must be abandoned. A variety of party names was suggested—Federal-Republican, Republican-Federal, American-Republican, American-Whig, True-Republican, True-American, even Democratic-Federalist. "Names are influential things," a Connecticut Federalist declared, "and much has been effected by the term Democratic Republican. In my opinion it is time to leave this distinction.

All of this contrasted sharply with the convictions and the conduct of old-school gentlemen. The two generations regarded each other with a mixture of friendly disapproval, impatient frustration, and outright distrust. Older men dismissed the younger generation as a pack of popularity-hunters. The younger generation in turn anathematized its elders—"Sere and yellow leaves falling around us," Verplanck called them—for their failure to adapt themselves to political reality. . . .

Generally speaking, the gentlemen of the old school did not think well of electioneering. They hoped that the people might be trusted to choose the "best men" without regard to promises or favors. This political ideal permeated American politics during the eighteenth century. Many colonies and states passed laws against electioneering. . . . In Virginia, as realistic a politician as James Madison expressed his "extreme distaste" for "any step which might seem to denote a solicitude" for office.

It is true, of course, that many eighteenth-century gentlemen who did not approve of electioneering were forced to practice it. In the plantation states, particularly, where "treating" at the polls was familiar from colonial days, an overscrupulous office seeker was often under-balloted. . . .

But it should be noted that even in the southern states, where electioneering was much more widespread than in the northern states, vote-seeking was restricted to a brief season of a few weeks. Except in turbulent times—during the Revolution or in 1788—it was the work of an individual or a small clique whose resources were limited. The ideals and the realities of eighteenth-century American politics combined to inhibit the growth of systematic electioneering on a large scale. Before the rise of the Jeffersonians, as [William A.] Robinson has written, "campaigning was the work of guerrillas rather than disciplined organizations."

During the 1790s the Jeffersonians revolutionized electioneering. By pooling their efforts they were able to sponsor campaigns far beyond the resources of the wealthiest individuals or the busiest of cliques. Their opponents complained bitterly of endless "dinings," "drinkings," and celebrations; of handbills "industriously posted along every road"; of convoys of vehicles which brought voters to the polls by the cartload; of candidates "in perpetual motion." It is true that all of these practices can be found on a smaller scale in pre-Revolution America. But there is a point at which a difference in degree becomes a difference in kind. The Jeffersonians reached this point and passed it during the 1790s. . . .

. . .By and large, older Federalists turned away from electioneering at the same time that Jeffersonians turned toward it. Samuel Goodrich later declared that gentlemen of the old school "did not mingle with the mass: they might be suspected of electioneering," which would have been "too degrading for them." A young Federalist in Massachusetts compalined that in his town "not a man had been spoken to about candidates" by gentlemen of his persuasion before the election of 1800. Even in New York, where Federalists were more active and better organized than anywhere else in the Union, one young man complained that they "were as usual supine till the eve of the election."

Many younger Federalists took a different view. Josiah Quincy [of Massachusetts] complained bitterly of the "cautious politicians" of the older generation, "men who neither devise nor execute." He denounced the "principles" which seemed "merely an apology of inactivity." A young Federalist in western Massachusetts, Loring Andrews, had written as early as 1798, "The fireside and the private circle will never answer to sit in judgment upon the abettors of French intrigue. Influential characters must be active—they must throw off all reserve—they must speak to the people in terms, and in tone, which the apparently all-important approaching crisis requires. They must not shelter themselves under any assumed masks. They must go forth among the multitude and personally discuss with them the things which appertain to their existence as an independent nation."

The young Federalists at first borrowed only the most gentlemanly techniques of the Jeffersonians. "You know, they use some weapons which we cannot condescend to," Henry De Saussure declared. The Jeffersonians had made extensive use of mass meetings in which voters came together, chose a chairman, reaffirmed the right of assembly, unanimously "nominated" candidates, passed a set of resolutions, and adjourned.

After 1800, the young Federalists borrowed this device and built their campaigns around it. In the few parts of the union where old-school gentlemen had used mass meetings during the 1790s, the young Federalists merely improved and enlarged. It was the custom of the "friends of government" in Boston, for example, to assemble in the Concert Hall on the eve of every important election. After 1800, however, young Federalists greatly expanded these meetings into "Grand Caucuses." By 1804 they found it necessary to announce that "the Concert Hall having been found too small, the Federalists have obtained leave to assemble in Fanueil Hall.". . .

The "nomination" of candidates in mass meetings, both Republican and Federalist, was often a sham, so transparently fraudulent that even the feeblest intelligence could penetrate it. As a consequence, more elaborate deceptions were developed. Mass meetings became "conventions," first in name and then in fact. Nominating committees were "appointed" by these meetings and supposedly responsible to them.

Also, meetings of Federalists multiplied rapidly on local levels, in part because large "risings" were so obviously fraudulent. In Salem, for example, a Republican noted in 1809 that "general caucuses [meetings] seem to have lost their reputation, and have yielded to ward and other sub-divisions. In this way, conversation is personal and the disposition of citizens is known." But ward and district meetings were supplements rather than substitutes for great mass meetings, which gradually grew greater. In 1808, the Boston Grand Caucus was attended by no less than four thousand Federalists! At a "New Hampshire rising" in 1812, two thousand spectators arrived in 500 vehicles to hear Federalist orators, including the "Godlike" Daniel Webster, "harangue" them from an open stage built specially for the purpose.

The gentlemen of the old school did not at first participate in significant numbers in the systematized electioneering of their younger colleagues; but gradually they began to join in. Gouverneur Morris noted in 1809 that he had gone "for the first time in my life, to attend a popular meeting in my county." The year before, a Federalist editor in Pennsylvania noted that at a mass meeting he noticed "the hoary heads of venerable freemen, some of whom had not attended a public meeting in twenty years." From South Carolina, in 1800, a young Federalist reported that "all the elderly men of high character whose health will allow them. . .will come out efficiently at the election," after having been prevailed upon to do so. . . .

The Federalists appear to have had difficulty mastering the strange art of "forensic degladiation," as one of them called it. At first they were sometimes awkward and ineffectual in their appeals to the people. In 1803, the young Federalist Roger Brooke Taney made himself the laughing stock of western Maryland by coming to Republican barbecues and bleating, "I am a *Republican!* A *true* Republican. My name is *Taney*—and now won't *you*—my *dear* dear fellow, won't *you* vote for me?" At first, too, some of the young Federalist stump speakers addressed themselves to "the understanding and not to the passions of the audience." But it was not long before they learned the value of a choice *ad hominem* or a sly innuendo.

The young Federalists understood that public meetings, barbecues, processions, festivals, political funerals, and other public celebrations were not sufficient in themselves to insure the success of a campaign. It was necessary for the party to go directly after the people, to seek out each Federalist voter at his hearthside. This was the primary task of local committees whose inception was discussed in the last chapter.

The detailed instructions and documents of Federalist committees in Connecticut in the Simeon Baldwin Papers shed much light upon the means employed by these busy little cells of federalism, and the energy, efficiency and thoroughness with which they operated. Town committees were responsible for maintaining lists of all freemen in their neighborhoods. Records were kept of their attendance at elections. All freeman who were not confirmed Jeffersonians were divided into groups of eight to ten each, and were personally visited by a member of the Federalist town committee or one of the "most active, sensible, and judicious men" in the town. County committees constantly exhorted their town committees to expand their efforts in extravagant language. One such message concluded, "The great object will be to get out the Freemen, and keep them out until the meeting is over. I will only add God save the Commonwealth."

The Federalist town committees were instructed to "pay particular attention to young men that are coming upon the stage, that they may be early engaged on the side of truth and sound principles." Each Federalist freeman was to receive a list of nominees, so that they might all "vote alike." Sometimes the Federalists put symbols on their tickets, as the Republicans had done—the arms of the union by the Federalists, and a shipwreck by the Republicans.

Federalists in other parts of the union seem to have been as active as those in Connecticut. [Samuel Eliot] Morison tells us that in Boston "vigilant ward committees made life miserable for stay-at-homes." In western Massachusetts, a leading Federalist politician, Henry Van Schaak, concluded a political letter somewhat abruptly with the following apology, "I write in great haste as my carriage is waiting. You will remember that my concern is business and not elegance. I shall go to every nook in the county where I can do the best good." In New York City, during the election of 1809, "every elector was served with a letter—enclosing a federal ticket, requesting him in polite terms to promote the federal candidates." The door-to-door campaigns of Federalist vigilance committees in Delaware were equally thorough. A Democratic editor immortalized one committeeman, "a big man with a cocked hat," who "was seen taking a squint over the *window curtains,* perhaps after *federal recruits!*" Republicans were sarcastic about these "once a year calls."

Federalists in many states made use of "runners," "riders," or vote distributors," "dapper young gentlemen," or "persons not uniformly of the first consequence," whose task it was to see that every vote! had a copy of the party ticket. John Carlyle Herbert of Maryland carefully instructed a neophyte Federalist in the tricks of the trade. "Remember, my good friend," he wrote, "that everything depends upon your retaining in all the districts a *Pay* if necessary—riders and agents who ought to be constables or young men aspiring to office—to mix with the people, circulate hand bills and papers, and if necessary to apply occasional pecuniary aid to political friends in need." The Federalist leaders in Salem, Massachusetts, had 120 vote distributors working, thirty in each ward in 1803.

Candidates themselves went out among the people shaking the horny hands of the laborers, inquiring after families they had never seen, listening patiently to questions and grievances, discussing issues and personalities. Federalists complained bitterly of this arduous and degrading toil, but they performed it nonetheless. Even Federalist candidates for the highest offices sometimes went out among the people. In 1808, James Ross, the Federalist candidate for the Pennsylvania governorship "made something of an electioneering tour in his own behalf." He spent two months on the one-week journey from Pittsburgh to Philadelphia, meeting people and making promises. Earlier in his career, Ross had sought to abolish religious tests and was charged with "atheism" by his opponents. In 1808, therefore, he made a special effort to "exhibit himself in places of worship where he has friends to introduce him."

Industry, ingenuity, and a non-too-strict sense of propriety characterized the young Federalists' adoption of electioneering techniques which had been used with such great effect against them by the Jeffersonians. Mass meetings, barbecues, stump speaking, festivals of many kinds, processions and parades, runners and riders, door-to-door canvassing, the distribution of tickets and ballots, electioneering tours by candidates, free transportation to the polls, outright bribery, and corruption of other kinds—all of these techniques and more were used by the young Federalists on a remarkably broad scale between 1800 and 1816.

PRESIDENT, CONGRESS, AND PATRONAGE

15   FROM   *Noble E. Cunningham, Jr.*
An Embodiment in the House?

When the Seventh Congress, elected in 1800-1801, met in December 1801, the Republican party had, in the President's words, "a very commanding majority in the House of Representatives, and a safe majority in the Senate.". . .

In the Eighth Congress [elected in 1802 to 1803], with the added representation following the census of 1800 and the admission of Ohio in 1803, Republican strength increased in both houses. Party strength at the opening of the first session stood at 103 Republicans and 39 Federalists in the House, 25 Republicans and 9 Federalists in the Senate. Although the party composition varied,

SOURCE. Noble E. Cunningham, Jr., *The Jeffersonian Republicans in Power: Party Operations, 1801-1809,* pp. 71-9, 81-5, 88-92 (Chapel Hill: University of North Carolina Press, 1963). Reprinted by permission of the publisher, The Institute of Early American History and Cultures and the author.

the Republican majority increased in each of the two subsequent Congresses which met while Jefferson was President. "In short," said Representative Jacob Crowninshield summing up the Republican position in Congress, "we are strong enough and have nothing to fear except from divisions among ourselves."

The first Republican-controlled Congress (the Seventh Congress) began by reversing the previous Federalist Congress on a number of issues, essentially carrying out the proposals which Jefferson outlined in his first annual message to Congress in December 1801. These included the abolition of all internal taxes, the repeal of the Judiciary Act of 1801, reductions in the army and in naval expenditures, and the initiation of a program to discharge the national debt in fifteen years. The liberal naturalization law of 1795, written by Madison, was also restored. Republicans sought to make their reversals of Federalist policies clear and to show that the change in parties was bringing changes of policies. That the voters were afforded visible evidence of the changes was suggested by one member who declared, on March 4, 1802: "On yesterday we passed the bill for the repeal of the judiciary system of the last session—59 to 37. On today we celebrate the anniversary of the triumph of republicanism—and on tomorrow we repeal the internal taxes. Thus, you see, this dreadful spirit—this spirit of innovation is going on." Republican partisanship was reflected in the appointment by the House of Representatives in December 1801 of a Committee of Investigation authorized to inquire into expenditures of public money by the several departments under previous administrations. Obviously designed to expose the misdeeds of the preceding administrations, the committee carried on the investigation throughout the session, presenting shortly before adjournment its report, which John Quincy Adams denounced as "highly exceptionable to every maxim of common justice and honor. This report was hurried through the House with as little regard to decorum as it was made."

Although the practice of party members in Congress choosing floor leaders had not yet become fixed, the role of party leaders in Congress gradually had become more and more important. In the Second, Third, and Fourth Congresses, James Madison had clearly acted as the leader of the emerging Republican party, and when he retired from Congress in 1797 his place was taken by Albert

Gallatin, who fulfilled the role of a minority leader during Adams's administration. When the Seventh Congress met in December 1801, with Gallatin now in the Cabinet, rivalry developed among Republican members over party leadership. As speaker of the House, the Republicans chose Nathaniel Macon, who had represented North Carolina in Congress since 1791. No aggressive leader, Macon had a consistently Jeffersonian record, no important enemies, and a certain unassuming honesty and integrity which made him a popular choice for the speakership. The speaker at this time enjoyed the extensive power of appointing standing committees, and in exercising this authority Macon played an important role in fixing the future party leadership in the House. To the chairmanship of the Ways and Means Committee, Macon appointed his close friend twenty-eight-year-old John Randolph of Roanoke, who had served but one term in Congress. The fiery and erratic Randolph and the plain and stable Macon were markedly unlike, but their personal and political friendship lasted a lifetime. In view of the close friendship of Macon and Randolph, it is unlikely that Jefferson had any influence in the choice of Randolph as chairman of the Ways and Means Committee. Macon also appointed another good friend, Joseph H. Nicholson of Maryland, to the Ways and Means Committee. Passed over by Macon was William Branch Giles, who had been Madison's chief lieutenant in the early Congresses and after resigning from Congress in 1798 had returned in 1801. . . .

Randolph, confessing "I feel myself pre-eminently embarrassed by the station which the partiality of the Speaker has assigned me," reported the majority "somewhat unwieldly" and admitted: "There is much want of concert and even discordance of opinion in the majority." As the session continued, however, workable Republican unity was established. By mid-January [the Federalist leader, Roger Griswold of Connecticut] who had hopefully predicted that Federalists could profit from Republican discord, despaired. "The majority finding themselves fast sinking into contempt by their ignorance and divisions," he wrote haughtily, "have as it seems determined to remedy one difficulty if they cannot the other, they have united." In March, DeWitt Clinton wrote from his seat in the Senate: "Our friends here are as well united as can be expected from so strong and so varied a majority." And Jefferson was satisfied at the end of the session that Congress had "carried into execution steadily almost all the propositions submitted to them in my message at the opening of the session." There is no reason to assume, however, that Randolph had as yet emerged as the party leader in Congress or as the administration's spokesman on the floor. On the other hand, the debates in the House indicated that Giles, whom one member called the *"premier* or *prime minister* of the day," acted as the principal House leader for the administration.

It was during this session that Jefferson confessed to Caesar A. Rodney the need for a leader in Congress. "We want men of business among them," he admitted. "I really wish you were here. I am convinced it is in the power of any man who understands business, and who will undertake to keep a file of the business before Congress and to press it as he would his own docket in a court, to shorten the sessions a month one year with another and to save in that way 30,000 D. a year." Rodney, at Jefferson's urging, had recently successfully challenged James A. Bayard for Delaware's seat in the House, and Jefferson was anxiously awaiting his appearance in the next Congress. It would hardly appear that Jefferson was satisfied with the potentialities of Randolph as the party leader in the House.

Giles did not return to the Lower House, and in 1804 he entered the Senate. In 1803, Samuel Smith [of Maryland] also transferred to the Senate, leaving Randolph the unchallenged Republican leader in the House. When the Eighth Congress met in October 1803, observers for the first time agreed that Randolph was the party leader of House Republicans. Federalists referred to him as "the democratic leader," "our great premier or self created democratic Manager of the House," and "the leader of democracy in the House of Representatives.". . .

Jefferson accepted Randolph's position of party leadership in the House, took him into his confidence, and attempted to make him the administration's spokesman on the floor. But Randolph's temperament hardly suited him for the role in which he was cast, and there is no evidence that he was ever popular with the President. While Randolph was at the height of his influence in Congress, Jefferson was writing to Caesar A. Rodney, who he had hoped would develop into a congressional leader, endeavoring to persuade him not to carry out his contemplated retirement after one term. Rodney yielded to the President's plea to run again, but Jefferson's hopes of his becoming a congressional leader were rudely exploded when Rodney was defeated in his bid for re-election.

Randolph, [meanwhile], came close to breaking with the administration over the Yazoo land issue. In 1802, Secretary of State Madison, Secretary of the Treasury Gallatin, and Attorney General [Levi Lincoln of Massachusetts] acting as federal commissioners, had obtained the agreement of Georgia to the cession of her western lands, with a reservation to cover unsettled private claims. In 1804, they proposed to Congress to settle these claims by a compromise settlement to claimants, mostly the Yazoo land companies which had purchased the Yazoo lands after their sale by the 1795 Georgia legislature. The rescinding of this sale by the 1796 Georgia legislature on the grounds of bribery had left their titles to the land in dispute. Although the commissioners denied the claimants' title, they proposed to reimburse them for their average expenditures on the ground that many were innocent parties who had purchased the lands from the original speculators unaware of the corruption of the legislature. To any such settlement Randolph was opposed; leading the opposition in the House to the compromise in 1804, he succeeded in postponing action until the next session. In 1805 when the matter came up again, Randolph's abusive denunciation of anyone connected with the compromise as sanctioning corruption. . .created much party discord. "There is a violent brakage among the Democrats," reported Representative Manasseh Cutler. "Johnny Randolph has been very much deserted by his party. . .he has violently attacked those of his party who had left him."

At the beginning of 1805, other congressmen were saying that Randolph's influence was waning. Samuel Taggart, a Federalist member from Massachusetts, noted in January: "John Randolph has. . .resigned his office of ruling the majority in Congress, for this substantial reason that he finds they will no longer be ruled by him. The candidates aiming at the honour of succeeding him are John W. Eppes, Joseph H. Nicholson, Roger Nelson, and perhaps others, none of which I think possess Randolph's abilities. One thing is certain the party at present seem broken and divided, and do not act with their usual concert." But Randolph was not to abandon his position of leadership until his break with the President in 1806, and he appeared in his most partisan role at the head of the House managers who conducted the impeachment proceedings against Justice Samuel Chase, whose removal for Federalist partisanship on the bench was sought by the administration.

Whether or not the deficiency of Randolph as a party leader or his conduct toward members of his own party in Congress would have led to the overthrow of his leadership without an open break with Jefferson can only be a matter of speculation, for in the Ninth Congress Randolph decided his own fate by deserting and denouncing the President who was also the head of the Republican party.

At the beginning of the Ninth Congress in December 1805, the President sought a secret appropriation of two million dollars for the purchase of Florida. Randolph was given a special presidential briefing, but he refused to support the proposal and led an unsuccessful attack upon it in the House. "Do not be surprised when you learn that the President's measures are not approved by our leader, J. Randolph," wrote Samuel Smith, and Federalist William Plumer rejoiced that "the *Great man* cannot render Randolph subservient to all his views."

Randolph's mounting hostility toward the administration reached a climax in March 1806, in the debate on the Gregg Resolution. This resolution, introduced by Pennsylvania's Andrew Gregg, proposed the suspension of the importation of British goods until England modified her policies in regard to neutral trade and impressment. Randolph began his attack on the Gregg Resolution on March 5 with a speech of two and a half hours, in which, amidst much argumentation little related to the issue, he proclaimed that the policy would lead to war and announced his own opposition to fighting for avaricious trading interests. The speech, said Senator Samuel Smith, was "replete with invective (the most severe that the English language can furnish) against the President, Mr. Madison and the Cabinet generally." Denouncing Madison's foreign policies, he read from a recent pamphlet on neutral trade by the Secretary of State and indignantly cast it on the floor. He denounced "back-stairs influence—of men who bring messages to this House, which, although they do not appear on the Journals, govern its decisions." He sneered that there was "no longer any Cabinet." "In truth," said Smith, "he astonished all his hearers, by the boldness of his animadversions on Executive conduct, the elegance of his language and the pointed and fine strokes of oratory. But he has left stings in the breasts of many, that never can be extracted."

Randolph's break with the administration was violent, decisive, and irreparable. The reasons for his action were less clear cut.

That Randolph was seeking to discredit Madison and to elevate Monroe to the presidency was widely recognized. "He is full in the spirit of electioneering for President," wrote Congressman Helms, "and to that object, in my opinion, he would sacrifice the best interests of his Country. His view is to bring in Mr. Monroe. . .perhaps he means to be Secretary of State himself the first four years, and then succeed to the Presidency." The suspicions that Randolph was looking to the election of 1808 were well founded; they can be substantiated from numerous sources.

[Yet, as] Randolph and others had suspected, the administration had not been satisfied with his leadership in Congress before he openly turned against the President. At the opening of the Ninth Congress in December 1805, Barnabas Bidwell, who had been an active Republican leader in New England and a member of the Massachusetts legislature, had rapidly emerged as a possible successor to Randolph. As a new member, he had made a strong impression in the House. "Mr. Bidwell is as smooth as the ocean unruffled by the slightest breeze," commented his colleague Samuel Taggart, after Bidwell's first speech from the floor in December 1805. Before long Taggart was writing home: "I believe neighbor Bidwell is now J[efferso]n's right hand man. Randolph does not spare to lash him." And Senator Plumer noted: "Mr. Bidwell . . .has much of the confidence of the President." Another member, reporting Randolph's irritation with Bidwell, explained: "The object of Bidwell is to be *primus inter pares,* immediately, and you may be assured, it will not be submitted to, with patience."

Bidwell had arrived in Washington enthusiastically recommended to the President by Levi Lincoln as "a uniform and warm supporter of the measures of the existing administration" and "a very useful acquisition in the national Legislature." That he had

caught the eye of the President was soon clear, and that Jefferson
had picked hlm fur hic majority leader in the House can also be
shown. When Bidwell considered declining to stand fur ro election,
Jefferson appealed to him to run again, explaining in a most
unrestrained letter that "there never was a time when the services
of those who possess talents, integrity, firmness and sound judgment, were more wanted in Congress. Some one of that description
is particularly wanted to take the lead in the H. of R. to consider
the business of the nation as his own business, to take it up as if he
were singly charged with it and carry it through. . . It is only
speaking a truth to say that all eyes look to you. It was not
perhaps expected from a new member, at his first session,. . .but it
would be a subject of deep regret were you to refuse yourself to the
conspicuous part in the business of the house which all assign to
you."

As a result of Jefferson's appeal, Bidwell reconsidered and agreed
to stand for re-election, explaining that his inclination to retire
had not been due to any dissatisfaction or discouragement but
because of family considerations. Obviously moved by Jefferson's
flattering letter, Bidwell expressed his appreciation of the President's confidence, but pointed out the difficulties in implementing
his suggestions. In a letter [equally revealing as that of] Jefferson,
he discussed the practical operation of the party in Congress,
explaining:

"I am constrained to say, you appear to expect more from my
exertions, as a member of the House of Representatives, than it
will be in my power to perform. The cant of back—stairs influence
has no terrors; but there are obstacles in my way. In every
legislature, the introduction, progress and conclusion of business
depend much upon committees; and, in the House of Representatives of the U.S., more than in any other legislative body within
my knowledge, the business referred to Committees, and reported
on by them, is, by usage and common consent, controlled by their
chairman. As the Speaker, according to the standing rules of the
House, has the appointment of Committees, he has it in his power
to place whom he pleases in the foreground, and whom he pleases
in the back—ground, and thus, in some measure, affect their
agency in the transactions of the House. From the connections and
attachments of the present Speaker, I have, at least, no reason to

expect to be very favourably considered, in his distribution of committee business. This circumstance, with others, of more importance, which I will forbear to mention, but of which I am deeply sensible, will prevent my acting a very conspicuous part. So far, however, as industry and moderate abilities may be relied on, I shall feel it a duty to be attentive to the business of the House; and, having had satisfaction of a cordial concurrence with the principles and measures of the Executive Administration, generally, it will be my happiness to give them the feeble aid of my support, both in and out of the House."

Bidwell's frank reply in stressing the importance of committee assignments and the power of the speaker reveals much of the workings of the House. It also clearly displays why Macon's continued attachment to Randolph, after the latter's defection, was to lead to his removal from the speakership. Although Bidwell was successful in his bid for re-election, he resigned from Congress in 1807 to accept appointment as the attorney general of Massachusetts, after Republican James Sullivan won the governorship of that state. Once again Jefferson's attempt to secure a party leader in Congress collapsed.

In 1807, Jefferson encouraged Wilson Cary Nicholas [of Virginia], who had earlier served in the Senate, to run for the House.

Never did the calls of patriotism more loudly assail you than at this moment. After excepting the federalists, who will be 27., and the little band of schismatics, who will be 3. or 4. (all tongue), the residue of the H of R is as well disposed a body of men as I ever saw collected. But there is no one whose talents and standing, taken together, have weight enough to give him the lead. The consequence is, that there is no one who will undertake to do the public business, and it remains undone. Were you here, the whole would rally round you in an instant, and willingly co-operate in whatever is for the public good. Nor would it require you to undertake drudgery in the House. There are enough able and willing to do that. A rallying point is all that is wanting. Let me beseech you then to offer yourself. You never will have it so much in your power again to render such eminent service. Nicholas complied with the President's wishes by consenting to stand for election, a movement which immediately aroused the suspicions of John Randolph, who confided to Monroe: "Mr. T.M. Randolph suddenly declines a re-election, in favor of Wilson Nicholas, whose talents for intrigue you well know, I presume." Nicholas was successful in his election, but, arriving as he did for the last Congress of Jefferson's tenure, he never became the kind of leader that Jefferson had in mind.

Jefferson had sought to develop a system in which the party would have an administration spokesman in a position of leadership in Congress, but various circumstances had interfered to disrupt the President's efforts. Only John Randolph effectively filled the post of floor leader, and he but for little more than two years. Although Jefferson had taken Randolph into his confidence, Randolph's position of leadership was not a result of executive influence, but rather the product of his own aggressiveness and his prominent position as chairman of the Ways and Means Committee. It is apparent that Jefferson would have preferred a sober man of business, such as Rodney or Bidwell, to the irascible Randolph, and he quietly worked to get and to keep such men in Congress. That his exertions were not more successful was not due to a lack of effort on the part of the President.

16 FROM *Carl E. Prince*

The Passing of the Aristocracy

Every difference of opinion is not a difference of principle. We have called by different names brethren of the same principle. We are all republicans: we are all federalists.

Thomas Jefferson uttered these celebrated words as the keynote to his first administration on March 4, 1801; and historians from Henry Adams to Marshall Smelser, with surprising uniformity,

SOURCE. Carl E. Prince, "The Passing of the Aristocracy: Jefferson's Removal of the Federalists, 1801-1805," *Journal of American History,* LVII (Dec. 1970), pp. 563-575.

have accepted the inaugural statement as a reasonable reflection of the President's policy toward the Federalists whom he found entrenched in the first federal civil service. . .[Indeed], the treatment of Jefferson's dealings with the Federalists—a foundation stone upon which any interpretation of Jefferson the President as politician must rest—has remained consistent in placing the seal of moderation and forbearance on the third President's conduct.

"Moderation," in fact, was just the word Henry Adams used, adding that Jefferson "could afford to make few removals for party reasons." Historians writing on the subject since Adams have agreed that moderation was more or less an accurate characterization of Jefferson's patronage policies. . . .

Two historians have attempted systematically to measure Jefferson's management of the civil service he inherited. Carl Russell Fish more than half a century ago came closest to a precise measurement when he totaled up the removals from the service listed in the *Executive Journal of the Senate of the United States.* Fish concluded that once Republicans occupied a due proportion (50%) of the federal offices at Jefferson's disposal, the President, who rarely turned anyone out for political reasons alone anyway, ordered removals to cease; thus, under the first Democratic-Republican President, Fish concluded, "the character of the civil service was really not much changed" and only "technically" can one assign to Jefferson any responsibility for introducing a "spoils system" in the federal service.

In a more detailed and comprehensive, though not a quantitative analysis, Noble E. Cunningham, Jr. was in general agreement. . . .Cunningham recognized that "under the pressure of Republican demands and the influence of continuing Federalist opposition, the President's earlier sentiments of moderation and conciliation had undergone noticeable modification." Yet, he added, "on removals his practice and policy were not so clear cut," and Cunningham concluded that "in general, Jefferson tried to steer a middle-of-the-road course" with regard to removals— "less moderate" at first, "more cautious later." All other modern historians of the Jeffersonian Republican epic agree that the Virginian followed a reasonable line with regard to his treatment of the Federalist civil service.

The implications of these appraisals collectively are that Thomas Jefferson placed a premium on the right to political opposition, fixed on a policy resting mainly on merit, did not stoop to sweeping the political stables clean, and avoided the pitfalls inherent in politicizing the civil service. Jefferson, in short, was no Andrew Jackson when it came to spoils.

The fact is, however, that Jefferson's patronage policy during his first term was as decisive as it was thoroughly partisan. Removals in one form or another for purely political reasons constituted the backbone of his effort to break the Federalists' power, particularly that party's stranglehold on the sensitive and politically potent second line United States offices operative in the states.

Jefferson had to deal with 316 second level offices in 1801: the inferior federal judges serving during good behavior and not normally subject to removal, the federal law enforcement establishment in the states, the customs department, the internal revenue service, and some civil appointments in the War and Navy departments. Using the figure 316 as an accurate base, reflecting as it did the total number of federal offices in the states subject directly to presidential discretion, it is possible to draw some conclusions that differ markedly from the present conception of Jefferson the party leader in the White House. The founder of the Virginia Dynasty in one way or another forced out 146 incumbents (46%), at least 118 (37%) of whom can be identified as hardcore Federalist party cadre occupying the most politically useful offices in their respective states in the gift of the President. It is probable that virtually all of the 146 deposed officeholders were Federalists; however, for the sake of accuracy only those will be counted who can positively be singled out as Federalists who engaged actively in partisan activities even while holding office in the 1790's and through the election of 1800. That is to say, men who electioneered, chaired party meetings, engaged in Federalist propaganda activities, coordinated political activities, or sought systematically and continuously to use their official positions and private influence to affect the politics of others in their respective communities. 118 of the 146 who were replaced in Jefferson's first term, then, clearly conform to this definition of Federalist party activist. . . .

Before examing in detail Jefferson's treatment of his civil service, an explanation of technique is in order. Historians have heretofore accepted as complete the removal statistics derived from the *Executive Journal of the Senate of the United States*. The fact is that for strategic reasons President Jefferson did not always list as such men removed from office for political causes. It was not only indelicate to do so in many cases; it might also have proved politically damaging to the Jeffersonians inasmuch as the *Journal* was a public document available to members of both parties. Publication of the real statistics would have confirmed Federalist allegations about Jefferson's partisanship. That an individual was indeed removed, however, was sometimes noted on his private file folder in the archives of the State Department, where all personnel files were kept. . . .Moreover, several Federalist incumbents disclosed publicly for political reasons, or privately, either pleading for their jobs or writing to associates, that they were forced to resign under threat of being turned out—an either/or situation for them. Jefferson used this tactic extensively, although no one has ever taken note of this fact. Finally, even though a few Republicans appointed early on by Jefferson had to be otherwise provided for (they almost always were), Jefferson sunk more than a few Federalist ships when in 1802 he forced the repeal of the Judiciary Act of 1801 and "reorganized" the Internal Revenue Service. In sum, not only were many Federalists displaced by a variety of devices, but invariably the party men occupying the key posts were the ones to go.

Undoubtedly the federal circuit and district judges filled the most prestigious offices open to presidential appointment in the states. The U.S. Circuit Court, although long on the drawing boards, had not been created until the final days of the Adams administration. . . .The Federal District Court was established in 1789. Its judges, like those in the Circuit Court, usually served in their home states and were appointed during good behavior. These posts, then, were not ordinarily subject to presidential dismissal.

The fact that these United States judges were not normally removable did not deter Jefferson. . . .[He] found thirty-two inferior federal judges presiding in their respective states when he took office. The Virginian set out to establish a political balance in the federal judiciary. The most difficult and controversial result of Jefferson's efforts in this direction involved the impeachment and removal of United States District Judge John Pickering of New Hampshire. Although allegations that by 1803 Pickering was either mentally ill, perpetually drunk or both were probably true, efforts to impeach and convict him. . .were inspired by political considerations. . . .At Jefferson'e instigation Pickering was impeached and removed by the Senate.

Other District Court judges suffered similar though less spectacular fates. . . .The President [meanwhile] made no appointment of his own to the new Circuit Court, presumably because he knew it would soon be abolished. The repeal of the Judiciary Act of 1801 shot down fifteen more judges at one time, all presiding in the United States Circuit Court and all of them Federalists.

All in all, then, of thirty-two existing inferior federal judgeships, Jefferson found thirty of them in Federalist hands; three serving in the District Court were dropped for essentially political reasons. Fifteen more Federalists fell by the wayside in 1802 as a result of repeal [of the Judiciary Act of 1801]. For all practical purposes, a sweeping political removal had taken place. Eighteen of thirty Federalist partisans were cleared from the bench by 1803, even though the President lacked the removal power in every instance. In view of these circumstances, the repeal of the Judiciary Act of 1801 must be seen as part of a larger effort to unhinge the Federalist party.

The President did possess the power to replace officials within the United States judicial substructure in the states, and here Jefferson acted decisively. That substructure contained some of the most politically oriented positions under the federal government. Recognizing this, the Virginian displaced thirteen of twenty-one U.S. attorneys, at least eleven of whom were Federalists. Two of those kept on, moreover, were Republicans. The new President then rooted out eighteen of twenty United States marshals in the states; at least thirteen of them were part of the Federalist cadre. Political power was a hallmark of both positions. The United States Attorney for a given state was responsible for prosecuting federal cases (for example under the Sedition Act), compiling evidence on all government suits originating in his state (e.g., violations of the customs laws), and farming out investigations to lawyers whose fees he assigned at his discretion. The marshal was charged with empaneling grand and petit juries for government cases (again, for example, in trials under the Sedition Act), and controlled extensive personal patronage in that he designated all assistant marshals serving outlying areas of his state. Both positions, in short, were highly visible, highly political posts, hence the excessively large turnover. Only the sixteen United States District Court clerks, occupying politically innocuous offices, remained unscathed after Jefferson turned over the judicial establishment.

The upper reaches of the Internal Revenue Department consisted of sixteen supervisors of the revenue (one for each state) and twenty-one inspectors (three more were also acting supervisors); all of the latter served in the largest states. Of the supervisors, fifteen were Federalists. Six party men were released in 1801 and 1802 before Jefferson reduced the size of the department. Nine more Federalists found their offices cut from under them when Jefferson and Albert Gallatin reorganized the service in 1802. Twelve of the twenty-one inspectors whose positions were abolished can be identified as Federalists also. All twelve were either displaced prior to the reorganization of the service, or dislodged by the cutback.

Of the 146 customs officers subject to presidential removal, Jefferson replaced fifty, of whom forty-one can be identified as Federalists. The President dropped all but one of the customs officers in the ports of New York and Philadelphia, where party activity abounded. All five New Jersey port collectors were turned out for the same reason. This was characteristic. Collectors occupied the most sensitive posts politically, in both large ports and small, because of their visibility and the patronage in the lower echelons of the customs at their disposal.

The story was much the same for New England. Portsmouth, New Hampshire was swept clean of its Federalist officers. The collectors of New Haven and Middletown, Connecticut were also removed. In Massachusetts, no less than ten politically active collectors were deposed; Boston Port, where politically motivated General Benjamin Lincoln of Revolutionary fame presided, remained untouched, however. To the southward, four Maryland collectors (excluding Baltimore), six Virginia customs collectors (including those at Alexandria and Norfolk) and the collector at Savannah, Georgia all fell victim to Jefferson's patronage axe. The political significance of the removal of these Federalist collectors was enhanced because the forty one known Federalists who were dislodged had at their disposal some 271 other customs positions in the lower reaches of the service; most of these, naturally, also passed into Republican hands.

The major moderating circumstance introduced first by the President and later by the historians to justify those removals to which Jefferson admitted was the presence of cause—apart from that of Federalist activity. Undefined "misconduct" or "delinquency" was often the reason he or his subordinates assigned to justify dismissals. Of the sixty-nine removals Jefferson acknowledged, only nineteen, he said, could be considered political. Because of the complexity of defining just cause for dismissal from office, it poses a tough problem to tackle. First, it must be said, inference to the contrary in Jefferson's own analysis notwithstanding, in the archival annotations only political reasons were offered as cause for the bulk of the replacements. Only seventeen cases turn up in which causes other than purely political were disclosed, discounting of course instances where offices were legislated or reorganized out of existence.

In four of these seventeen cases, excessive drink was the assigned cause for vacating public offices—a valid justification by almost any standard. Yet examination of individual circumstances in each case indicates that unsubstantiated allegation was enough to move the President to action. . . .

Perhaps the most revealing case of removal for excessive drink was that of Joseph Tucker, Collector of Customs at York, Maine. He was represented to the Jefferson administration in 1803 "to be constantly drunk and incapable of business, and a violent *federalist.*" Tucker was turned out. The town of York immediately convened a town meeting and voted 106 to 0 to refute the allegation and to support Tucker's appeal for restoration of his office. Every selectman in town, in addition to the citizens, added his signature to a petition to the President that concluded by pointing out that Tucker "has held every office in the Town of which he would accept." In spite of this impressive denial of the charge, no further investigation was made and a Republican succeeded to the collector's post. It is clear that even a legitimate cause for dismissal was usually bound up with a man's politics; in some cases, moreover, it is evident that the "cause" was simply a pretext to remove a Federalist—whether or not the reason given was susceptible of proof.

Four more of the seventeen dismissals for cause involved the charge of toryism during the American Revolution. . . .However. . .the credibility of that stigma as a reason for dismissal was impaired by Jefferson's appointment of three tories who happened to be Republicans even as he dismissed four loyalists who were Federalists. [For example], Woodbury Langdon of New Hampshire was designated U.S. Navy Agent for the district of Portsmouth in 1801. Langdon, an active Tory for at least part of the Revolution, was also brother to influential Jeffersonian United States Senator John Langdon. . . .

The remaining nine cases of dismissal for cause involved allegations of neglect of duty or financial peculation—charges which may have been accurate, although in each instance the allegations were coupled with denunciations of the officer's political activism. Whatever the cause, whether it involved a purely political removal, politics in combination with another allegation or abolition of the office by statute, the 118 Federalists shared in common an active involvement in the leadership of their party in their particular states.

That Federalist leadership, in turn, constituted an American social and political aristocracy—an elite that Jefferson meant to unhinge from the sources of its political power. Nor was it a dying aristocracy. Indications are that the bulk of the removals involved younger Federalists, in their most productive years, who continued to engage the Jeffersonians long after 1801. Of the fifty-seven dismissed Federalists whose ages could be uncovered, forty-one (35%) had been born after 1750, while only sixteen (14%) were born before that date. It was not, in David H. Fischer's words, primarily "old school" Federalists who suffered but the younger, "second generation" party men who felt the cutting edge of Jefferson's patronage axe.

There can be no doubt that the displaced, by several definitions, constituted a slice of an authentic and very old American gentry. Of the eighty whose occupations could be determined, no less than seventy (59%) were engaged in callings of the highest stature in the nation. Thirty-six lawyers, twenty-four merchants and ten more who were ship's masters, physicians, bankers or planters fell by the wayside. Of the eighty, only ten (8%) were artisans or farmers. The appelation "wealthy" applied to at least thirty-five (30%).

In determining elitism other criteria also apply. Some sixty (51%) of those removed were either scions of long-standing aristocratic American families, or kin to such families. Forty-three (36%) fall into the first category and seventeen (14%) into the second. At least twenty-five (21%) were graduates of ranking American or English colleges. The officers corps of the Continental Army contributed at least thirty-two (27%) of those dropped. . . .Among the deposed elite also were thirteen (11%) former members of the Congress of the United States, and nine (8%) members of the Continental Congress.

Jefferson, in sum, not only moved decisively in ridding his administration of Federalists, but he also took on a very impressive and influential political and socio-economic hornet's nest. Taking all the elite categories enumerated above as a whole and after discounting any overlapping of categories, there were at least eight-eight (75%) who could claim elite station among the removed Federalists.

Thomas Jefferson in his first years in office was clearly touched by the burdens of power and responsibility; he was affected, perhaps, far more than either he and his followers cared to admit, or historians have heretofore acknowledged. Examinations of what he said have proven somewhat misleading. To arrive at a more accurate assessment of his political leadership in the White House, it is important to take into account more substantially what he did. The President was not the moderate party leader in power that historians have depicted him. Far from binding the ideological wounds of the nation, his actions defined more clearly than ever the dichotomy prevailing within the existent two-party structure of American politics. In some ways the emergent party system stood out with much greater clarity after 1800 than it had in the 1790's. . . .In short, the changing of the guard, though not for the reasons offered by Henry Adams, can indeed be viewed as "the revolution of 1800."

It was a revolution in the sense that it led to the systematic elimination of a long-standing, heretofore well anchored aristocracy from the second line of the federal government. That the

Republicans perhaps replaced the old with a new, modified aristrocracy does not detract from the purposeful and degrading damage inflicted on the existent elite, representing as it did many of the oldest and best established families in America. The operation performed on the old guard at the second level of government, where it thought itself secure despite the election returns of 1800, can be viewed in two ways that are not necessarily mutually exclusive. On the one hand it marked the beginning of the end of Federalist power in the several states by seriously impairing the power base and prestige of the entrenched Federalist leadership; on the other hand, it hastened the advent of the second generation Federalists' reorganization of the party structure by stirring them, perhaps for the first time, to greater machine-oriented efforts.

In any case, Jefferson's sweeping removals policy, and its shattering impact on the American elite, marked a decisive turning point in the maturation of the first American party system.

PART FIVE
The Weakness of Party, the Remoteness of Party

The first party system was not to last. The Federalists suffered general debilitation; and the Republicans, in part because they had no effective competition, fell victim to internal divisions. By 1817 the Federalists had collapsed as a national formation, although state party structures persisted in some form as late as the mid-1820s in a few states. Meanwhile the Republican phalanx disintegrated into squabbling fragments and ceased to act as an effective force some time between 1817 and 1819. Yet the name persisted: indeed, nearly every later, working politician made use of it.

Intraparty factions first appeared among the Republicans during Jefferson's presidency, on the national scene and in crucial states like New York, Pennsylvania, and even Virginia. By and large Jefferson was able to cope with factional strains or, at least, to keep them from totally rending party ties. When sharper divisions appeared as James Madison took over in 1809, however, the new President proved unable to match his mentor's skill. The result, as William Nisbet Chambers observes, was a progressive weakening of the party fabric. Division went still further under Madison's successor, James Monroe, who tried to act in the spirit of the Era of Good Feelings, although that spirit was, perhaps, more rhetoric than reality. He deprecated party and, in effect, eschewed party leadership. Before long, the national Republican party had come unravelled.

Meanwhile, especially after the Republican triumph of 1800, the national government appeared as a somewhat distant power. Remoteness of the governed from the government, and "the isolation of the governors from the governed"—this, according to James Sterling Young, was the situation after the "city" of

Washington was created as the nations new capital. Perhaps Young exaggerates: surely Hamilton's fiscal program and issues like the undeclared war with France, war taxes, and the Alien and Sedition Acts were matters of public concern. So also, presumably, were undertakings such as the Louisiana Purchase in 1803 or Jefferson's controversial embargo on overseas commerce, which touched many citizens directly and sapped Jefferson's prestige and power. Yet it is true that the matters that affected most Americans directly, where they lived and worked, were in the compass of state rather than national authority. There was also little evidence of continuing exchange between the Washington politicians and their constituents, Young argues, partly because the newly contrived village on the Potomac was itself remote from the established lines of commerce and communication. To the degree that the national government seemed far away, so did national parties.

In the Washington of the Virginia dynasty, moreover, members of Congress tended to fall into state and sectional groupings. Men from the same area tended to live together in a particular boardinghouse or "mess". (There were few private homes.) In these rendezvous, political talk predominated, and congressional messmates came to share similar views on public questions: in effect, the close-knit, almost isolated messes appeared to serve as demifactions. Their role was particularly significant during the presidencies of Madison and Monroe, in part because of the near absence of presidential or party leadership of the sort Jefferson had provided. To the weakness of party and to the remoteness of party was added another impulse for the fragmentation of party.

As party declined in the national arena, parties in the states tended to fall away. There were some exceptions, as Richard P. McCormick notes, such as the "Bucktail" and "Clintonian" state parties in New York, and the Federalist hangovers in Massachusetts and Pennsylvania. Popular involvement in national politics remained low, however, until a new, national party constellation took form. Not until exciting political combat in the late 1820s through the 1840s focussed attention on the contest for the presidency did most voters become deeply involved—particularly so with colorful hero-candidates like "Old Hickory" Jackson and "Old Tippecanoe" Harrison. New, broadly democratic extensions of the suffrage, the fact that by 1832 every state except South Carolina chose presidential electors by popular vote, and the impact of skilled campaign managers and exciting mass appeals, all joined to bring unprecedented numbers of citizens into the game. The result was a highly organized, increasingly competitive second American party system that was far more vigorous than the first; and it rallied far more party workers as active participants as well as voters. It was, indeed, a kind of early participatory democracy, although it came more and more under the control of its newly professional political managers.

This "new brand of politics" set basic forms of party action that were to persist with little change for more than a century to come, although the second party system also broke up after 30 years and gave way to its successors. Yet under it all, the first party system of Federalists and Republicans had opened the door and had started the process.

THE VIOLENCE OF FACTION

17   FROM   *William Nisbet Chambers*
Political Parties in a New Nation

The Federalists under Hamilton had marked the trial to party development, and the Republicans under Madison and Jefferson had followed it, hacking out on their own additional paths toward a popular party. In their rivalry the parties had cut the clearings for a two-party system, and had substantially completed the work within a quarter-century of the time the new American nation had declared its independence.

Yet the original American party system was not to endure. The Federalists. . .torn by factional dissension, fell away after the year of Jefferson's triumph. Before long the Republicans were also entangled in thickets of factionalism, and within a decade of Jefferson's retirement [in 1809] they had all but disappeared. New

SOURCE. From *Political Parties in a New Nation: The American Experience, 1776-1809*, by William Nisbet Chambers, pp. 191-197. Copyright c 1963 by Oxford University Press, Inc. Reprinted by permission.

men were faced with the task of cutting paths for new parties, although they were able to benefit from the work of their predecessors.

While failure may bring failure in party interaction, as it had for the Federalists, success does not always bring success. The very triumph of the Republicans, their position as a dominant party, the fact that their dominance drew around them an increasingly broad combination of interests and segments of opinion, the variety of leaders they attracted—all contributed to the outbreak within the party of what Madison years before had called "the violence of faction." In the post-Jefferson era the rivalries of politics—rivalry for power and between personalities, rivalry of interests trying to win recognition for their demands in public policy, rivalry for office and patronage—occurred more and more within the Republican party, rather than between Republicans and Federalists. Thus intraparty struggle and contention came to replace interparty competition on the high road of political conflict. As the old two-party system gave way, the successful Republicans were beset by difficulties of a sort which often threaten a single supreme party.

The ironic consequence was that the party Madison had helped to found was to be torn apart on the harsh thorns of faction, and it was Madison's role to head the party as it neared its destruction.

Intimations of trouble came as the President-elect planned his cabinet in 1809. Although the able and experienced Gallatin seemed the obvious choice for secretary of state, resistance to his appointment soon appeared. It began with a clique gathered around the influential Smith brothers of Maryland—Samuel, in the Senate, and Robert, Jefferson's former Secretary of the Navy—and their Virginia kinfolk including Wilson Cary Nicholas, together with other allies. The movement also drew support from some of the associates of George Clinton in New York and from many of the Pennsylvanians who had personal or patronage quarrels with Gallatin, including William Duane and Michael Leib, who was now in the national Senate. The Smith clique and the anti-Gallatin "Invisibles," as they came to be called, advanced Robert Smith for the State Department post. As a strong party-and presidential-leader, Jefferson had moved adroitly to contain or divert such factional forces. The question now was, what would Madison as the new party leader do?

Unfortunately for the Republican party's future, he capitulated. He appointed the mediocrity, Smith, and granted patronage to the Smith clique and the Invisibles, thereby offending the friends of Gallatin. Yet two years later, Madison was forced to remove Smith and replace him with Monroe, this time offending those he had previously gratified and confirming them in opposition. Soon insiders were commenting on the conflict between Madison's "Cabinet" group and the Invisibles as intraparty factions. Meanwhile, the faithful Gallatin remained at the Treasury.

The whole futile episode was symptomatic of Madison's address to such party problems. Always hoping for harmony, he proved reluctant to fight, surprisingly inept in handling appointments and patronage to strengthen party cohesion, and often irresolute; once an able Congressional party leader, he seemed increasingly lost in the problems of party as he became more and more absorbed in the trying problems of state. Thus he lost the direction of affairs at the capital and even within his Administration itself. By 1811 Washington Irving was commenting, "Poor Jemmy!. . .[he is] a withered little apple-John." In the same year John Randolph commented more acidly, "He is President de jure only; who exercises the office de facto I do not know."

The harassments of clique maneuvering were soon followed by open, forest-fire factionalism. The Republican combination had been stretched again and again to encompass the variety of interests in the nation, and it had been further enlarged with the settlement of the New West beyond the Allegheny Mountains. From Kentucky and Tennessee, and from frontier areas of New York, South Carolina, and Georgia, came increasingly strident expansionist demands for American acquisition of Canada and Spanish Florida. Angered by new blows to American interests in British-instigated Indian raids on the frontiers and with one eye on recurring British depredation of American commerce on the high seas, extreme nationalists from the West pressed for war against Great Britain. Meanwhile, partly in reaction to such forces, the Congressional elections of 1810 had swept 63 of the 142 members of the previous House of Representatives out of office, most of them Republicans. Many were replaced by Republicans of a new generation, who were expansive, untameable, and aggressive in their views and style, particularly when they came fresh from frontier districts. When Congress convened in 1811 these new members found their leader in the adroit, magnetic Henry Clay of Kentucky, gambler, political manager, and orator, whom they elected Speaker in his first term of office . . .Old "Invisibles" were thus replaced by "Young Republicans" in the forefront of faction. Such men as Peter B. Porter of western New York and the brilliant John C. Calhoun of the Piedmont area of South Carolina soon joined Clay as factional leaders.

No country bumpkins in politics, the Young Republicans moved promptly to consolidate their power in the House. They breathed new life into the Congressional caucus and generally controlled it. They also encouraged the development of standing committees, knowing that Clay as speaker would appoint their chairmen; and by 1814 the committee system had become the dominant force in the chamber. Thus effective power was exercised not by the President. . . but by factional Congressional leaders working through the speakership, the caucus, and the committees. The Young Republicans had less influence in the slower-to-change Senate, but even there they had allies and sympathizers led by the imposing William H. Crawford of Georgia. A distinct Congressional as opposed to presidential wing of the Republican party had emerged, and it intended to have its own way.

The new men continued to press their extreme nationalist demands. In the House, John A. Harper of New Hampshire reiterated the call for American acquisition of Florida as the intent of "the Author of Nature," and in the Senate Crawford of Georgia banged his desk and demanded Canada. By the spring of 1812 the most extreme of the Young Republicans were so stridently demanding war against Great Britain that Randolph's epithet for them was appropriate—"War Hawks," he dubbed them. In domestic affairs Clay and his allies pressed for what Clay grandiosely called the "American System," a program which ultimately came to include high protective tariffs, internal improvements at Federal expense in roads and canals (particularly in the West), a national bank, and a continuing public debt. This system was entirely too neo-Hamiltonian, too bluntly aimed at developing the nation and particularly the New West on a capitalist basis, to be anything

but anathema to purist, seaboard "Old Republicans." Yet it was
more than just Hamilton over again, for in the period of Madison's Administration this earlier version of a "people's capitalism"
appealed to far broader segments of the population than Hamilton's original program had. All told, the policies of the Young
Republicans gave their forest-fire faction great resources of power.

Once again, Madison's stance was uncertain. Trying to find
wise roads of policy, he nonetheless felt unduly pressed and was
inclined to accommodate the Young Republicans as far as he
could. Moved by other issues and the failure of other policies as
well as by War Hawk pressures, he finally called for a declaration
of hostilities against Great Britain and thus undertook the War of
1812. The year before, while the President had remained silent,
Congress had refused to recharter Hamilton's bank, but in 1816,
faced indeed by new conditions as well as new pressures, Madison
signed a bill which Congress sent to him establishing a second
Bank of the United States. Clique, factional, and group pressures
had produced sharp intraparty divisions in the roll-call. . . .Thus,
for the man who had fought Hamilton, the irony of factional strife
was compounded by the irony of neo-Hamiltonian measures in
Republican dress. Meanwhile, John Marshall on the Supreme
Court was on the way to fixing Hamiltonian conceptions in the
corpus of broad constitutional interpretations by the judiciary.

The Young Republicans had become the effective driving force
in politics. Yet they were only an intraparty faction contending
with other factions, and not a party. They lacked the formal
control of the executive which would have enabled the voters to
hold them fully responsible for the conduct of government, and
they could not present options to the electorate as a party. The
United States had come almost, but not quite, to a stage of one-
party government accompanied by intraparty factionalism. The
Republicans were virtually unassailable in positions of [national]
power despite Federalist residues [in the states]; the party was the
nearly universal vehicle for the representation of interests and for
political participation; most of the important conflicts of national
or sectional interest groups were more and more fought out within
its boundaries; and the great issues were shaped and settled mostly
by men who carried its name. In this sense, the Republican
formation exhibited certain parallels with later dominant parties

in new nations of the twentieth century. More than one faction fought within its ranks, and the party as a whole and its presidential leadership were unable to subdue or control factional forces. Yet in this situation, the Young Republicans were the major innovative element within a loose and divided party, but not a controlling one.

Thus, other factional surges had appeared in the election of 1812, and the trials of Madison-Job seemed without limit. The Young Republicans supported Madison in a late Congressional caucus in 1812 only after they were convinced that he would call for war. Yet many "Old Republicans," the Smithites and others in the Middle Atlantic and New England states, and the mercantile and shipping elements who had found their way into the extended Republican coalition, all opposed what came to be called "Mr. Madison's War." The consequence, again fostered by local and personal motivations as well as by national conflicts, was a movement for young DeWitt Clinton of New York as a presidential candidate, and the top Clintonian leaders joined in a secret conference with certain Federalist leaders to effect a tacit fusion for the election. "Poor Jemmy" was beleagured on both sides in 1812, by Young Republicans crying up the war, and by seaboard and mercantile forces crying it down—nearly all of them working under the name Republican! As a result, democratic choice for the voters was confused. Suggesting opposition to the war in some areas and support for it in others, the carefully ambiguous Clinton carried all of the New England states except Vermont, along with New York and New Jersey and five Maryland's eleven electoral votes. The original Clintonian strategy had been to hold these bastions and to strike for Pennsylvania's twenty-five electoral votes; and if fusion had succeeded in Pennsylvania, he would have won the day. As it was, Madison pulled through only by the margin of his victory in the Keystone State.

In the long run, however, the often discouraging war had also stirred patriotic sentiments. Finally the hostilities seemed to end in a blaze of glory when frontier troops under Andrew Jackson of Tennessee smashed British regulars led by Lord Pakenham at New Orleans. The outbursts of joy and patriotic hallelujahs swept the nation. One result. . .was an additional setback for the Federalist party, many of whose leaders had opposed the war, while some in

New England had even verged on treason. The Republican star climbed higher, and despite a factional struggle in an ill-attended Congressional nominating caucus in which Monroe barely won over Crawford, it continued to shine benignly in the presidential election of 1816. In consequence, Monroe bested Rufus King [the last Federalist candidate for the presidency] by an electoral count of 183 to 34. Events, however, were to show that his triumph was not in fact a gain for party.

A DISTANT POWER

18   FROM   *James Sterling Young*
            The Washington Community 1800-1828

Almost no one, it seemed, could find anything flattering to say about the capital in the Jeffersonian years. To travelers and diplomats from abroad, the showcase of the new nation was a gigantic monument to pretension, the confirming evidence that the Americans had attempted something beyond their capacities. "Voila un Capitol sans Ciceron; voici le Tibre sans Rome," said one visitor, and recited Thomas Moore's famous gibe about "This embryo capital, where Fancy sees/ Squares in morasses, obelisks in trees." Among Americans, also, the capital became a butt for jokes, and poking fun at Washington became something of a national passtime. "The national bantling" it was dubbed, the benighted and ungainly offspring of the nation. "The Federal city is in reality neither town nor village," crowed a Philadelphia editor; "it may be compared to a country seat where state sportsmen may run horses and fight cocks; kill time under cover and shoot Public Service flying. . . .There sits the President. . .like a pelican in the wilderness, or a sparrow upon the housetop."

SOURCE. James Sterling Young, *The Washington Community 1800-1828,* pp. 41-2, 44, 48, 26-28, 30-35, 98-102, 104-5 (New York: Columbia University Press, 1966).

And to those whom ambition and desire for service brought to Washington, it became "this city which so many are willing to come to and all [are] so anxious to leave." For the utter desolation that public disinterest had made of their environment was not the least of those "splendid torments" that Jefferson called the political vocation: Washington was an ever-present reminder to the men in power of the low esteem in which power was held.

The stage for the national drama was a vast construction site "bearing the marks of partial labour and general desertion." Two unfinished stark white citadels towered above the terrain from hilltops on opposite shores of a dismal swamp, more like ruins amid the fallen fragments of their own stone than new and rising edifices. Where monuments had been planned, brush piles moldered and rubbish heaps accumulated. Where majestic avenues were to sweep, swaths of tree stumps stood, rough quarried stones marking the intersections. Where houses were to be, barren hillocks, stripped of vegetation, rose like desert islands amid a sea of bogs and marshes. . . .

Against this desolate landscape the halls of government stood as Henry Adams was to see them decades later, "unfinished. . . . white Greek temples in the abandoned gravel-pits of a deserted Syrian city." To the men who occupied them they brought no reassurance of dignity and little comfort. . . .

Such was power's home in a nation wedded to the doctrine of the sovereignty of the people: a pleasureless outpost in the wilds and wastes, manned for only part of the year, abandoned for the rest.

To what may this fiasco be attributed? Why was the public response to the national government as a social presence so markedly different from the public response to the Constitution when it had been presented for ratification? Poor location and bad publicity obviously contributed. Clearly, too, mismanagement and miscalculation by those responsible for planning and building the capital were factors. Their ineptitude was so great and their miscalculations so enormous, indeed, as to raise the question of how deeply motivated these men were to make the seat of government the vital center of the nation. Would men wholly committed to the ideal of a flourishing metropolis for the governmental residence have isolated the government from all the established centers of national life, chosen a wilderness for its site, and placed it beside a river dubiously navigable where it was not wholly impassable because of rapids and falls. . . . Would they have failed to use the most obvious source of funds for making the capital a showplace—the public treasury?

It could be that the rulers, in staking the success of the venture upon a favorable mass response, were utterly blind to the possibility that a free citizenry may also be a politically indifferent citizenry. It could be, too, that they entertained a colossally distorted notion of their own importance in the public eye. But it would be less surprising, in explanation of their "ineptitude" in making a capital, to find some measure of ambivalence concerning the objective itself: to find, among men of republican sentiments, something less than a wholehearted dedication to the task of centering the life of the nation around the seat of national government.

It is doubtful, however, that the most unambivalent commitment and the most expert management on their part would have significantly altered the course of events that made such a dismal travesty of their magnificent visions. . . . Fundamentally, it would appear that the government itself was an institution of too little significance to attract population and wealth to its residence.

For the government of Jeffersonian times was not, by any candid view, one of the important institutions in American society—important as a social presence or important in its impact upon the everyday lives of the citizens. It was, for one thing, too new, an unfamiliar social presence in a society whose ways of living and whose organization of affairs had developed over a century without any national governmental institution whatever: a society of preeminently provincial attachments. Even those who came to Washington as elected persons must have found the places of power dubiously rewarding, for they resigned in extraordinarily high numbers to continue their office-holding careers elsewhere than in Washington. And if the seats of power themselves held so little attraction, what incentive was there for ordinary citizens and free men to pay for places below the throne?

The early government was also a small institution, small almost beyond modern imagination. In 1802, the twelfth year of its existence under the Constitution, the entire task force of national government—army, navy, marines, and all the civil establishments abroad and in the continental United States—numbered considerably fewer persons than the federal employees now engaged in Indian affairs. . . . The official members of the governmental community, two years after they arrived in Washington, numbered 291—roughly one-fifth the size of a single army battalion, including a bureaucracy not as numerous as Congress. . . .

Small size indicated slightness of function. Two months of the year spent in Washington were sufficient for the Supreme Court to perform its business. Congress ordinarily worked only after the harvest season and before spring planting. There was no Chief Executive and no cabinet at the seat of government for almost three months of each year, usually; and the government of the nation was entrusted largely to the chief clerks of departments during the summer season.

What government business there was was not, most of it, of a sort to attract any widespread, sustained citizen interest. As a task force, the early government was an organization principally of warriors and revenue collectors. Approximately 95 percent of its manpower was assigned to military functions and to the production of revenue, with more than four times as many personnel engaged in servicing the national treasury as were assigned to all other civil functions of government, foreign and domestic. How attenuated were its functions as an instrument of social control is indicated by the fact that there were more people making the law than enforcing it, Congress outnumbering the whole law enforcement establishment including marshals, district attorneys, and federal courts. As a provider of services and benefits to citizens, the national government was insignificant, unless one counts the postal service, which was then looked upon, and actually was, a profit-making enterprise of the Treasury Department. And a government could not be very much more than a debating society which had, at its headquarters, a Congress larger than its administrative apparatus.

Almost all of the things that republican governments do which affect the everyday lives and fortunes of their citizens, and therefore engage their interest, were in Jeffersonian times *not* done by the national government. The administration of justice, the maintenance of law and order, the arbitration of disputes, the

chartering and supervision of business enterprise, road building
and the maintenance of transportation systems, the schooling of
the young, the care of the indigent, even residual control over the
bulk of the military forces—these functions fell principally within
the province of state and local governments to the extent that any
governmental bodies performed them. An institution whose involvement in the internal life of the nation was limited largely to
the collection and delivery of letters could hardly have been
expected to be much in the citizens' consciousness, let alone to
attract many to Washington. . . .

Small wonder, then, that the public response to government as a
social presence was so very different from the public response to
the Constitution when it was presented for ratification in 1787-
88. . . .

As cogently as the causes of this failure, its consequences compel
attention, namely, the isolation of the governors from the governed.

"Monks in a monastery," the rulers at Washington called
themselves. It may have been hyperbole with respect to their
behavior, but it was realistic with respect to the situation of a
governing group consigned to sylvan solitude. Theirs was the lot of
governing a society which they could neither see clearly nor know
well except in the fragments of it that were their own home
constituencies. They did not even know the shape of the new
entity called the nation in 1800, in so basic a matter as precisely
where its frontiers lay; they had no inventory of national facts
upon which to draw except what the tax revenues and the
decennial census revealed about the state of the country. They had
no observers and listeners among their own people as they had in
the capitals of Europe. To remind them of what and whom they
were governing, nothing representative of American life was visible
in their surroundings. They failed to encounter, when they were
governing, those critically important surrogates of the popular will
that bother but also aid and inform the men of office today—the
citizen delegates trooping to the capital full of opinions to air and
demands to press, the quasi-official cadres of reporters, lobbyists,
pollsters, professional party politicians, bringing the officeholders'
constituencies within talking distance and providing clues to the
public mood. . . .

One wonders, therefore, whether eliciting the interest and attachment of a free people was not a more fundamental problem for the newly established government than the problem of deciding policy for a free people. To observers of emerging nations today the problem of building citizen interest and support for a new governmental establishment is not unfamiliar. Neither was it unfamiliar to Alexander Hamilton when he wrote pessimistically, in *The Federalist,* No. 27, about the capacity of "government at a distance and out of sight" to "interest the sensations of the people."

"The more citizens are accustomed to meet with government in the common occurrences of their political life, the more it is familiarized to their sight and to their feelings, the further it enters into those objects which touch the most sensible chords and put in motion the most active springs of the human heart he observed, the greater will be the probability that it will conciliate the respect and attachment of the community. . . . The more it circulates through those channels and currents in which the passions of mankind naturally flow, the less will it require the aid of the violent and perilous expedients of compulsion."

One can thus detect, in the isolation of the governmental community and the citizen indifference which gave rise to it, a major operational problem for the rulers of the new nation and a major dilemma for a representative government founded on the doctrine of popular sovereignty: How to "interest the sensations of the people" and "avoid the violent and perilous expedients of compulsion"? The Jeffersonian era dramatized rather than solved this problem of a distant and isolated government. . . .

Within the. . .governmental community, members segregated on the basis of branch affiliation. Within the congressional subcommunity, members segregated principally on the basis of sectional affiliation. Legislators had a decided aversion to sharing their mess table, their living quarters, and their leisure hours with colleagues from regions other than their own and much preferred to live in groups restricted to men having approximately the same geocultural affiliation. . .While most members saw to it that they had at least one companion from the same state in their mess, and while it was not unusual for a substantial portion of a state's delegation to gather under the same roof, few boardinghouse groups were comprised exclusively of members from the same state, and only rarely did an entire state delegation reside together. Living in regionally mixed groups was preferred to living alone, but the truly cosmopolitan groups were few. Even when members from distant parts of the country formed a mess group, most often the group was dominated by a majority from the same state or region.

Ranging in size to as many as thirty members in one mess, the typical boardinghouse group was, then, a party of southerners or of westerners or of New Englanders, a conclave of New Yorkers, Jerseymen, and Pennsylvanians, or perhaps "a sett" of Virginians and Marylanders. Within the congressional messes, Senators and Representatives mixed freely, bridging in their extraofficial life their constitutional separation in official life. The young mixed with the old, the newcomers with the old-timers, the lawyers with the farmers, and the farmers with the merchants. But politics did not, for all this, make strange bedfellows on Capitol Hill. For these were not the important differences among sojourners in power, outward bound to the varied cultures of a new nation. In a heterogeneous society most members sought provincial companionship, setting themselves apart from men different in their places of origin and differently acculturated. They transformed a national institution into a series of sectional conclaves.

Characterized by the distinctive manners and customs of its region, "each mess was an organized community in itself," with social distance maintained between the messes. Within the group, "our association on the floor, and. . .in our. . .lodgings, led to the reciprocation of friendships which remained intimate and cordial during the continuance of our mutual Congress life"; outside the group, "intercourse for the most part was polite, but cold and general." Encounter between members of different fraternities appears to have been limited largely to the five or six hours daily when everyone was assembled for work in the Capitol, and even then some accounts suggest that mess groups selected a bloc of neighboring desks on the floor itself. Visiting between the messes after hours was said to be infrequent. "The company is good enough," wrote a Representative of mess life, "but it is always the same, and . . .I had rather now and then see some other persons."

If not avoided by choice, visiting was discouraged by lack of privacy and space within the boardinghouses. "Our not being able to have a room each is a great. . .inconvenience," wrote one of the party activists in the early Congress. Guests would have to be received in the common room or parlor, a "hot oven full of senators and representatives" and "abounding with noise and intrusion," where the members assembled after dinner to play cards, tell tales, talk over the events of the day, "& then for politics".

[The] members who lived together, took their meals together, and spent most of their leisure hours together also voted together with a very high degree of regularity. One hundred sixteen roll call votes in the House of Representatives [in the years 1807, 1809, 1816, 1828, and 1829] were selected for study, and the voting behavior of each boardinghouse group on each roll call was analyzed. In almost 75 percent of the resulting 2,657 cases analyzed, messmates voted unanimously or with only one dissenting vote within the group. . . .In only 11 percent of the cases did as many as one third of the members of a group dissent from their group's vote.

Moreover, boardinghouse fraternities voted as blocs quite independently of the size of the majority vote in the whole House—independently, it would therefore appear, of the voting cohesion of the majority and minority parties in the House. Since a unanimous vote in the whole House would necessarily mean perfect unanimity in all boardinghouse groups, it might be expected that, as the size of the House majority increased, so would the incidence of agreement significantly increase within the subgroups that were the congressional messes. If such had been the case, the high incidence of group agreement shown in [roll call votes] would be less significant as a measure of the importance of these groups in the voting structure of the early Congresses. [The data shows] that this was not the case, however, on the 116 roll calls analyzed here. Boardinghouse groups voted as blocs on the closely contested issues in the House just as they did on the less controversial issues, decided by a large majority margin. Moreover, the incidence of bloc voting by messmates not only failed to rise but tended to decline slightly as the size of the majority vote in the whole House increased. The more evenly divided the House sentiment and the more closely contested the issue, the greater, apparently, was intrabloc "discipline" and the reliance upon messmates for political cues.

The voting performance of the congressional messes clearly suggests, then, that legislators looked for policy guidance, as they did for companionship, to colleagues from the same locale or region, and that these intralegislative fraternal associations were influences of major significance upon the members' voting behavior. This is not to assert that boardinghouse fraternities were the only source of guidance nor the only politically significant associations on Capitol Hill. But no other grouping of legislators was institutionalized in the social structure of the congressional community. No other grouping was reinforced by such constancy and intensiveness of social interaction between the members as the boardinghouse fraternities. And. . .for no other type of grouping was political conformity asserted to be the moral obligation of the individual member, nor individual deviation from the group attended with such drastic sanctions. . . .

THE COLLAPSE OF PARTIES

19 FROM *Richard P. McCormick*
The Second American Party System

The failure of the Federalists to sustain themselves as a national
party brought about the decline and eventual disintegration of the
first American party system. Many explanations of the unsuccessful career of the party could be advanced. It could be argued that
they lacked effective leadership, that they espoused unpopular
policies, that they were too strongly identified with the Northeast,
and that they represented the outmoded survival of aristocratic
traditions in an increasingly democratic society. There is certainly
merit in all of these contentions. But in an admittedly narrow
political context, the failure of the Federalists could be attributed
to the fact that they did not appreciate the importance of the
contest for the presidency in the American party system and did

SOURCE. Richard P. McCormick, *The Second American Party System: Party Formation
in the Jacksonian Era,* pp. 26-31. (Chapel Hill: University of North Carolina Press,
1966).

not fully exploit the potentialities of that event. Except in 1812, they virtually permitted the presidency to go to the Republicans by default; they made no determined, imaginative, or farranging efforts onbehalf of their poorly selected candidates.

The Republicans, once they had won the presidency and dominance in Congress, obviously possesed many advantages over their rivals. In their efforts to achieve power, they had been stimulated to organize an offensive against the Federalists and had created the rudiments of party machinery and a strong *esprit de corps* among their adherents. . . . Of decided importance, too, was the availability of the successive members of the "Virginia dynasty"—Jefferson, Madison, and Monroe—whose prestige was sufficiently great to forestall the kind of crippling conflict over the succession that was to ruin the party in 1824. The early formation of the Virginia-New York alliance, despite the occasional restiveness of the junior partner, gave the party a strong base in the Middle States and by moderating its sectional character conferred on the Republicans a national appeal that the Federalists could not match.

Indeed, the party ultimately became the victim of its success. As the Federalists weakened, both at the national level and within individual states, the Republicans found it increasingly difficult to maintain the fiction that unity and discipline were essential to the party. Unity was destroyed by factionalism, partisan zeal subsided, party machinery fell into disuse, and even party identification came to have little meaning.

A sursory survey of the condition of parties in the states before the presidential election of 1824 reveals the extent to which the first American party system had disintegrated. There were fourteen states, exclusive of South Carolina, in which at some time politics had been organized on the basis of competition between Republican and Federalist parties. In only five of these—Maine, Massachusetts, New Jersey, Delaware, and Maryland—were elections still being contested in terms of the old party designations. In seven other states—Vermont, New Hampshire, Connecticut, Rhode Island, Pennsylvania, Virginia, and North Carolina—the Federalists had either "retired" from electoral combat or had become so weakened through loss of members or fusion with Republican factions as to leave the Republicans virtually unchallenged. Only in New Hampshire and Pennsylvania were there major contests in elections, and these were between rival factions within the old Republican party. Elsewhere, elections were dull affairs that gave unopposed victories to Republican candidates, except when local personal rivalries aroused voter interest. Two other states—New York and Ohio—can be treated as special cases. In New York after 1820 the Bucktails and the Clintonians [in affect, state parties] represented a distinctive type of party formation that had no counterpart elsewhere. In Ohio few vestiges of partisanship survived; even the Republican party had all but lost its identity and politics was conducted essentially on a personal basis. . . .

The first American party system had been influenced by the constitutional and legal environment that prevailed during its formative years. By 1824, when we can begin to observe the formation of the second American party system, that environment had altered, and the party system was to reflect these new conditions. Most important of all was the gradual change that had taken place in the method of choosing presidential electors. In 1800 electors were chosen by the legislatures in ten states; in only two states were they chosen by popular vote of the state at large. By 1824 only six states still clung to the legislative coice, and after 1832 South Carolina was the only state that did not choose electors by popular vote from the state at large.

The significance of this change in the method of conducting presidential elections has been too little appreciated. The general adoption of the popular, state-wide voting procedure gave a popular dimension to the presidential contest, created or enhanced the need for state party machinery, weakened the political authority of legislative caucuses, occasioned the development of national party conventions, and made the presidential election the dramatic focal point of American politics. What most differentiated the Jackson elections from those in which Jefferson was involved was this change in the method of choosing electors.

Between 1800 and 1824, too, suffrage qualifications were liberalized in several states—notably Connecticut, New York, New Jersey, and Maryland—with the result that nearly all adult white males were eligible to vote by 1824 in presidential elections, except in Rhode Island, Virginia, and Louisiana. Voting was also facilitated by refinements in election machinery. In most states polling units—or election districts—were reduced in area in order to enable voters to exercise their franchise with a minimum of inconvenience. *Viva voce* voting, with its lack of secrecy and its cumbersomeness where long slates of officials had to be elected, was steadily replaced by the ballot, and—indeed—by the printed ballot. As state constitutions were revised, more and more offices were made elective, instead of appointive. The custom of holding state elections at different times from presidential elections persisted, however, and before 1832 only New York held both elections on the same day.

Whereas the first American party system had been effectively limited to fourteen states—in four of which the Republicans quickly achieved lopsided dominance—the second American party system would embrace twenty-three states by 1835. In the sense, then, of geographic and sectional extension, the party system acquired a new dimension, and the difficulties inherent in operating national parties was compounded. One of the remarkable achievements of the second party system was to be the extension of party politics to these newer states.

In many other respects, the political environment had altered between the age of Jefferson and the age of Jackson. As long as politics could be managed informally, without the agency of elaborate party apparatus, those who were recognized at the time as "the gentry" wielded decisive influence. But the role of the gentry declined when politics was organized on a party basis. . . .

The new brand of politics was to differ from the old, then, in part because of these changes in the environment. Politics was not to be conducted under the same conditions in 1830 as in 1800. The sum effect of new conditions was to give an increasingly popular tone to politics. Campaigns and elections assumed the aspect of folk festivals. Candidates and voters indulged themselves in a moving, engrossing, and satisfying dramatic experience. As many foreign observers astutely noted, politics in the United States filled a need that was met in many European nations by the pomp, ceremony, and pageantry of the great established churches. The opportunity to participate in spectacular election contests gave the humble citizen a sense of identification that was intensely important to him. No account of American politics can ignore this "dramatic" appeal, although we have scarcely begun to appreciate its peculiar force and its powerful consequences.

SUGGESTIONS FOR FURTHER READING

A basic bibliography of the first American party system may be gleaned from the source citations that are given at the

beginning of each selection in this book. In every case, the scholar involved has more to say than it was possible to include here.

In addition to these materials, the older historiography is distinguished by Charles A. Beard's *Economic Origins of Jeffersonian Democracy* (New York, 1915), which is still stimulating despite some errors and its overemphasis on the conflict of economic interests. In the basically Beardian mode, consult also Wilfred E. Binkley, *American Political Parties: Their Natural History* (New York, revised edition, 1962), a general survey, and state studies such as Dixon Ryan Fox, "The Decline of Aristocracy in the Politics of New York," *Studies in History, Economics and Public Law,* Columbia University, LXXXVI (New York, 1919), and Walter R. Fee, *The Transition from Aristocracy to Democracy in New Jersey 1789-1829* (Somerville, 1933). A work that stands between Beardian and more modern analysis is Manning J. Dauer's *The Adams Federalists* (Baltimore, 1953), which also contains a wealth of information and useful statistical material. A pre-Beardian account of American party history to 1900, M. Ostrogorski, *Democracy and the Organization of Political Parties,* two volumes (New York, 1902), is lively and still useful, although it gives limited attention to the Federalists and to the first Republicans. Another later, general survey, Herbert Agar, *The Price of Union* (Boston, 1950), contains a pointed treatment of the events involved in the ultimate disintegration of the Jeffersonian Republicans.

Two modern, groundbreaking studies of the early American political culture within which parties arose have come from

Bernard Bailyn: *The Origins of American Politics* (New York, 1967), and *The Ideological Origins of the American Revolution* (Cambridge, 1967). See also Gordon Wood, *The Creation of the American Republic* (Chapel Hill, 1969), which carries much of Bailyn's approach into the 1780s. These studies should be compared with J. R. Pole's treatment.

The new wave of research into the first party system can be dated from Joseph Charles, *The Origins of the American Party System* (Williamsburg, 1956), a set of insightful essays supplemented by some early quantitative data. See also the earlier inquiry by Eugene Perry Link, *Democratic-Republican Societies, 1790-1800* (New York, 1942), which is ancillary to parties as such, but relevant. Critical junctures in the Federalist career are treated, along with Dauer, by Stephen G. Kurtz, *The Presidency of John Adams: The Collapse of Federalism 1795-1800* (Philadelphia, 1957), and Shaw Livermore, Jr., *The Twilight of Federalism: The Disintegration of the Federalist Party, 1815-1830* (Princeton, 1962), which buries the party, but slowly. A developmental analysis characterizes Seymour Martin Lipset's volume, *The First New Nation: The United States in Historical and Comparative Perspective* (New York, 1963), which includes a long, introductory chapter on early American politics. Analitical and developmental approaches to party formation as such an be found in William Nisbet Chambers, "Parties and Nation-Building in America," in Joseph LaPalombara and Myron Weiner, *Political Parties and Political Development* (Princeton, 1966), and in William Nisbet Chambers and Walter Dean Burnham, eds., *The American Party Systems: Stages of Political Development* (New York, 1967), which also carries the party story into the 1960s. In the first of these volumes the introductory and concluding chapters by LaPalombara and Weiner are useful for a comparative view; in the second, see especially the essays by Paul Goodman and Richard P. McCormick, as well as the ones by the editors. In different veins, two very recent accounts are useful. One is Donald H. Stewart, *The Opposition Press of the Federalist Period* (Albany, 1969), which provides a panorama of what the Republican newspapers had to say about issues, politics, and politicians. Another, Linda K. Kerber's *Federalists in Dissent: Imagery and Ideology in Jeffersonian America* (Ithaca, 1970), deals with the problems the

Federalists faced as they sought to maintain their conservative ideology in an era of emergent popular democracy.

Several state and regional investigations, most of them recent, provide extended materials for intranational comparative analysis. Among the most useful are Richard P. McCormick, *The History of Voting in New Jersey: A Study of the Development of Election Machinery 1664-1911* (New Brunswick, 1953), Carl E. Prince, *New Jersey's Jeffersonian Republicans: The Genesis of an Early Party Machine, 1789-1817* (Chapel Hill, 1967), and Staughton Lynd and Alfred F. Young, "After Carl Becker: The Mechanics and New York City Politics, 1774-1801," *Labor History*, V (Fall 1964), 215-224, for the crucial middle states. The South is explored in two studies by Norman K. Risjord, *The Old Republicans: Southern Conservatism in the Age of Jefferson* (New York, 1965) and "The Virginia Federalists," *Journal of Southern History*, XXXIII (November 1967), 486-517, and in a book by Lisle A. Rose, *Prologue to Democracy: The Federalists in the South, 1789-1800* (Lexington, Kentucky, 1968). See also, although they are not strictly in the party ambit, a vivid portrayal of early Virginia politics by Charles S. Sydnor, *Gentlemen Freeholders: Political Practices in Washington's Virginia* (Chapel Hill, 1952), and Anthony F. Upton, "The Roads to Power in Virginia in the Early Nineteenth Century," *Virginia Magazine of History and Biography*, LXII (July 1964), 259-280, on the persistence of the Old Dominion's political forms. The second "big" state of the time, Massachusetts, is the focus of James M. Banner, Jr.'s *To the Hartford Convention: The Federalists and the Origins of Party Politics in Massachusetts, 1789-1815* (New York, 1970), an incisive treatment of the Commonwealth's political nabobs and their later frustrations.

Fresh, modern research on party development in other states is badly needed. The field is open from New Hampshire or Connecticut to Maryland or South Carolina. Moreover, these studies may be on their way, and some may, indeed, appear before this book is in print. If they are informed by sophisticated analysis and build on previous research in a cumulative, comparative fashion, they will be immensely useful. We shall not only know more about early state parties but also more about national parties and politics.